MACKBEE

Mary M. Mackbee: Educational Leader for All Students of Today and Tomorrow

As told to and Written by Jane L. Sigford

COVER DESIGN

BY COURTNEY DANIELSON
PHOTO: Aaron Lavinsky
By agreement with Minneapopls Star and Tribune

Paperback ISBN 9798854971065

Ebook ISBN

DEDICATION

For Mary—Dedicated to my Parents Mildred Grey and Reynard Morrell
Thanks for giving and teaching me independence.

For Jane—to my sons and daughters-in-law
Mark and Shannon Thibert
Joel Thibert and Courtney Danielson (my favorite graphic artist)

And to my granddaughters Audrey and Stella Thibert

TABLE OF CONTENTS

PREFACE vii
INTRODUCTION ix
CHAPTER ONE 1
  Minnesota—Land of the 3 M's 1
CHAPTER TWO 4
  Beginnings 4
    High School 27
    Xavier University 30
CHAPTER THREE 56
  Central High School 56
CHAPTER FOUR 74
  Firsts, Awards, Accomplishments 74
    Breaking Barriers—Firsts 75
    Awards 75
CHAPTER FIVE 78
  Challenges and Hurdles 78
    Poverty 78
    Sexism 83
    Racism 90
    Relationships and Marriage 105
    Marriage 106
    First Year as Central's Principal 117
    Death of a Child 121
    DEmotion that became a PROmotion 124
CHAPTER SIX 133

Values and Assets	133
Believes people are important	133
Justice	141
Listener and being non-judgmental	141
Intelligent	143
Sense of Humor	144
Humility	144
Generous	145
Ethical	146
A Fighter	147
Problem-Solver	148
Conclusion	150
CHAPTER SEVEN	151
Leadership	151
Sexism	151
Mary's definition of Leadership	158
Abstract definition of Leadership	162
C.Cryss Brunner's Research	167
Friendships	180
Privacy	181
Discarding Myth	182
Sexual innuendos	183
Life Circumstances of Community	189
Life Circumstance of Challenge and Personal Characteristics of courage	191
Curiosity and Creativity	192
Doing more than one thing at a time.	199
Practical Leadership in Action	207
Conclusion: It's about the Person	211

CHAPTER EIGHT 213
  What made Mary Mackbee such a good Leader 213
CHAPTER NINE 217
  Currently...217
BIBLIOGRAPHY 222

PREFACE

I was fortunate to be an Assistant Principal to Mary Mackbee at Central High School in St. Paul, Minnesota. Because of her example and leadership style, I learned a great deal about administration, people, race, and life in general. I found her to be one of the most ethical administrators I ever had the pleasure of working with.

I am not the only person who recognizes her skills. Mary Mackbee is recognized as a leader across the state of Minnesota and even at the national level, especially with her leadership in the International Baccalaureate community. Under her leadership the IB program at Central High School was a stand-out in the numbers of IB diploma graduates and its overall success in academics, particularly because Central is an urban high school. Urban high schools are not often seen as academic leaders; however, Central is recognized for its excellence for academics, offerings for all types of learners, and for its artistic and athletic programs.

IB was not the only stand-out program at Central High School. Central, the oldest continuously operating high school in Minnesota, is a community high school embedded in a neighborhood that can proudly say that there are neighbors who can claim three generations of graduates. Plus, it attracts students from other districts, including suburban districts, and develops students who go on to serve their community in so many ways. Central can boast of Rhodes scholars, mayors, Olympic athletes, judges, legislators, and many others. It provides opportunities for studies in many areas ranging from auto mechanics to the arts to music production to theater to dance to strong academics to strong athletics. In recognition of its overall excellence Central High School proudly earned the distinction of being a nationally recognized Blue Ribbon School.

Mary Mackbee was its leader for 25 years. She led, supported, and fought for this school. She mentored teachers, administrators, and students. She supported this local community.

One of her gifts to Central, St. Paul, and Minnesota, in general, was her acumen in leading a multicultural school and community. She taught us all about honoring differences and building a school that celebrated different cultures. She modeled how a leader honors a culture and looks forward to what could be.

Because, I, like many others, learned so much about leadership from her, I wanted to share this story so others can see leadership in action.

INTRODUCTION

Mary Morrell Mackbee, like many others, has a fascinating life story that has is an exemplar of an inspirational life well-lived. She is a role model for so many leaders of all kinds, including women and people of color.

Mary worked in the St Paul School District for over 50 years in many roles—teacher, assistant principal, District level Director, and high school principal for 25 years, which in itself is a feat considering longevity is not often seen in school administrative jobs, particularly now post-COVID when burn-out is apparent.

When Mary finally agreed to let me write her story, I saw the book as having two parts: her life story and her leadership style. I originally thought I would have two distinct sections, but I realized that the two topics are intertwined--leadership style is built upon life experiences and cannot be separated from that. I had to integrate the two. Leadership is as much, or more, about the person in the role as it is about the techniques described in textbooks or seminars. Leadership is a person.

Therefore, I started with Mary's story to see how her leadership developed because of her life. But I also needed to address the concepts of leadership from a research perspective to be examined under the cultural, sexist, and racist practices in operation because that determines attitudes and practices that have been, and still may be, in operation throughout our society. It's necessary to examine all of this to see why Mary's style can be utilized as educational leader for the future, not just about the past. Research both supports her style and her style informs leadership because it is the opinion of this author that research is too often focused on the "what", as opposed to the "who". Leadership is not a solitary "thing"; it is as multi-faceted as an apeirogon which will be described in later chapters.

I also realized that there is a dearth of actual books from practicing leaders who are able to describe their lessons and applications in a real-life, non-theoretical framework so others can improve their leadership skills. Stacey Abrams', a representative to the House of Representatives and the first African-American female to be supported by a national party to run for a governorship which, in this case, was for the state of Georgia. Her book provides thought-provoking suggestions for leadership with unique perspectives. I hope Mary's story can be another such resource.

Ultimately, leadership is a person, a composite of life experiences, education, values, beliefs, successes, learning experience (failures), grit, kindness, and self-awareness. Leadership cannot be explained in isolation without including the person(s) involved and the situation where the leadership is exercised.

That's why Mary's story is so important.

CHAPTER ONE
Minnesota—Land of the 3 M's

Many people recognize Minnesota as the Land of 10,000 lakes, but it is also the state of the famous, or not so famous, 3 M's---Minnesota, Mining, and Manufacturing and Mary Morrell Mackbee. As a major industry in Minnesota, 3M has been a leader in developing some products that have become famous, including post-it notes, adhesive tape, audio-visual equipment and media, medical and dental products, and safety products such as reflective coatings and signs.

As a major educational leader in Minnesota, Mary Morrell Mackbee has also been an innovator as a teacher and administrator in St. Paul for over 50 years, contributing to the lives of thousands of students, families, and other educators.

One rarely hears of a Southerner adopting the frozen north as their homeland, but Mary M. Mackbee did exactly that. Originally, she left her native Louisiana, not because of Minnesota's lakes, beautiful summers, winter skiing, or lutefisk, but because of love—of a boy, and stayed because she found a place which she grew to love and where she came to be beloved.

This is Mary's story, the story of a Black woman who was able to take advantage of some educational opportunities for herself and where she was able to create a multitude of educational opportunities and experiences for hundreds of adults and students.

This story will be told differently. Most biographies or memoirs are chronological to witness how a child grows into a memorable adult. Mary's story is more than that because it is not just about her remarkable life; it is also about her leadership style which became an example to others and suggests skills for future leaders. What evolved from personal interviews with Mary were themes and topics that intertwine, overlap, and grew to create a story that is as complex as an apeirogon, a geometric shape with an infinite number of countable sides. (Apeirogon is the apt title of a novel by Colum McCann which put human faces to the complex issues underlying the Palestinian/Israeli relationship.) If one thinks about it, a human life is not just a linear timeline; it has lines which intersect, branch, cut other lines in two, fold back on some in intricate patterns that create new shapes, new directions, new patterns which are not easily described by a hierarchical framework. That is why this story—Mary's story—is also an apeirogon in how her life created many avenues, many branches, many stops and starts in her leadership style, proving that one's life is not simplistic, and neither is one's leadership pattern. If we want to understand how a person leads, we need to understand the person.

Because her words were captured in personal interviews, her words will be printed in **BOLD** so that one can "hear" and see her voice as though she is speaking to us directly. One will see how life experiences and leadership become an apeirogon.

A perfect introduction to Mary comes from her, not only in words, but in song, one that she performed as part of her campaign to run for high school student body president. She won, by the way. You might find yourself humming along to the melody of "Five Foot Two: Eyes of Blue.

> Five foot two, eyes of brown
> She will never let you down.
> Mary M's the girl for you
> Now if you run into a five foot two
> Running for prez, capable and all those things
> I bet your life that she's your girl.
> Oh, vote for her, vote for her,
> And just see what she can do.
> Mary M's the girl for you.

Let's begin....

CHAPTER TWO
Beginnings

It is typical to start someone's story with their birth and, perhaps, some information about their ancestry. Carolyn Mary Morrell was born on June 16th, 1944, in the Seventh Ward of New Orleans, Louisiana. The Seventh Ward is the third largest ward of New Orleans and was the home to Jelly Roll Morton, Allen Toussaint, and the made-for-HBO special "Treme." Her mother was Mildred Gray Morrell, who went by Mimi Gray; her father was Reynard Morrell. Mary has always used her middle name, instead of Carolyn.

Mary thinks her ancestors migrated to Louisiana from the Caribbean Islands. She did a genetic search through National Geographic which said that she was mostly sub-Saharan African, and European, with a little Asian in there. (2nd interview, February 17, 2023)

Mary never knew her grandparents. They had passed by the time she was old enough to remember. She did, however, know her great grandpa, who was actually her mother's grandfather. His last name was French, Renard, without a y. Interestingly, her father's first name was similar in that it was Reynard, but with a y. Her great-grandfather lived out of the city limits, in the country on St. John's Bayou. He lived in one of the shotgun houses that Louisiana is known for, with the biffy outback. The family would go there to see the person they called "Grandpa" even though he was really a great grandpa. He was a small man who was married to a little French lady. At that time Blacks could marry foreigners, even if they were white.

Gradually over time, where the great grandfather lived became the "place to be," the area began to be developed, and people moved in to build bigger homes. There was **Grandpa with his 3-room little shack. But nobody bothered him. He lived in a mixed neighborhood. He was the original person in that compound, so these big homes were just built around him and he just stayed where he was. Eventually, my brother Joe bought the property, I remember for $11,000. He** [great grandfather] **had 11 children, 9 boys and 2** girls [one was Josephine, Mary's grandmother] (2nd interview, Feb 17, 2023)

My mom's mother, Josephine, died when she was 31. I don't even think I was born yet. They (Mary's mom and "Grandpa's" children) **lived with my great grandpa because for a while Mary's mother was unmarried. My mom was raised by her aunts and uncles. The last sibling in my great-grandpa's family was born at the same time that my mother was born. Her aunt and she were the same age.**

The great-uncles all went into the military and almost all served in World War Two. My great-uncle Paul did join, but he was kind of "backwards", so they gave him an honorable discharge because I think he was illiterate. [One wonders if he was really backward or if had just never learned to read.] **There wasn't a school for Black kids out in the bayou. They'd have to come to town to go to school.**

I didn't meet any of my dad's grandparents. I met his sister and brother. They all have different names. My dad claims New Roads, Louisiana [located in Pointe Coupee Parish], **as his birthplace.** (2nd interview, February 17, 2023) New Roads is in one of the oldest settlement areas in Louisiana named after a "new road" the Spanish built in 1776 between the Mississippi and False River. (Louisiana travel, 2020) **I don't think my dad ever knew his father because he was orphaned young. His mother must have moved them to the cities. As he grew up, my dad worked in an Italian grocery** [the owners were white] **and lived in the French Quarter and went to the school named McDonough 15 which was a school for whites and is still operating. My sister-in-law became principal there later and found Dad's records, but his name wasn't Morrell. They had him under the Italian family name, passed him off as white so he could go to McDonough, otherwise he couldn't have. His attendance was poor. He never got past the second grade. Every year when he'd go back, they'd put him in the second grade. When he was 13, he dropped out completely.** (W-H dissertation, p. 26)

According to Mary, names in the South are always interesting. Her dad's siblings all had different last names. Her dad's last name was Morrell, but she had no idea where that name came from.

One of Mary's great grandfather's names on her mother's side was Renard. To carry on the tradition, Mary's son, Mateo, was Mateo Rey, after Mary's father, Reynard, because as she says, "**Rey is king, you know.**" On her mother's side the last name was from Wilfred Gray (2nd interview February 17, 2023). Her mother went by Gray. And brother Joe had two last names, Morrell and Prampin, which is another unique story.

A family tree

Eventually, the Morrell family consisted of Reynard Jr. (Mary's dad's son from his first marriage Mary's half-brother who never lived with them); Joe (actually, also Mary's half-brother, they shared a mother); Arthur; Mary; Raymond; Louis; Tommie; and baby sister Deborah. Mary's parents lived together as common-law husband and wife until Mary was out of high school, which was recognized as a legal marriage by the Napoleonic Code. Because Mimi worried that if her husband died or retired, she would be ineligible for any legal of health benefits, they were quietly married by a justice of the peace after 35 years of living and raising a family together.

We all knew that we were considered illegitimate in the South—I remember thinking that I was going into a vocation, perhaps being a nun—must have been a real short kind of a thought...and somebody said, "Well, you know, if you're illegitimate, you can't be a nun. I thought, well, that's one thing shot down. But that was OK—that may have worked to my advantage. (W-H dissertation, p. 29)

Joe's story is an interesting one, as I said earlier. As a young woman Mimi was a domestic worker to a white family. When she was 16 years old, she gave birth to Mary's oldest brother, Joe, whose father was the white homeowner who, according to Mimi, was planning to run away with Mimi. Was it or was it not a consensual relationship? Was she just protecting Mary from the truth? At any rate, Joe was born. On the birth certificate Mimi said Joe's name was Archille Prampin because it was a Mr. Prampin who was a friend of Mimi's, but not Joe's father. Sometimes Joe would call himself Joe Morrell and sometimes he would be Archille Prampin. (5th interview, March 21, 2023) He was light skinned. In fact, when he was in the military many assumed he was white. **He was white. He still is white. My mother was half white and his dad was white. So, he looks white. When he joined** the Air Force and he went to sign up, no one asked him his race. They wrote down white. So, he was stationed in Biloxi, Mississippi. And that was during the Civil Rights Movement. I got angry with him because he said they didn't know he was Black. He said, "Look, I'm in Biloxi, Mississippi. I either hang with people who I look like, and nobody knows the difference. Or, if I hang with Black people, they think I'm a liberal white person and, you know, I get in trouble.' In his whole service career, they thought he was white. (5th interview, March 21, 2023) Mary believed Joe was able to do things and go places that may have been off limits if people had thought he was Black.

In Mary's family of origin there were four last names—Gray, Renard, sometimes Prampin, and Morrell which, according to Mary, having several last names in a family is not unheard of in the South. Families are complicated no matter where they live. As Mary said, "**It's interesting and Joe calls it convoluted. In Louisiana there are different nationalities with a convoluted history.** (5th interview, March 23, 2023)

Four of her brothers served in the military. **There were no jobs, no money for college. Men got the G.I bill and could go on to college and technical college. Two younger brothers went to be welders because of the shipbuilding industry in Louisiana. Arthur was the only one who went to a four-year college and then became a lawyer. Both Tommy and Louis fought in Vietnam.**

Mary grew up in the segregated South. The 7th Ward was a segregated Black community with a mixed population, economically and professionally. One of Mary's neighbors was a lawyer and had a bigger house but, because of segregation, regardless of education or finances, Blacks of all professions lived in the same community. The only white person in the community was the Italian grocer who ran the corner store where everyone bought their groceries but he did not live in the community. Mary's family and others would walk to the store to get groceries. They did not own a car. In fact, Mary's mother never drove.

Mary's parents never owned their house until Mary was an adult. The typical New Orleans house is a "shotgun" house, meaning there are no hallways. You enter one room and must pass through each room to get to the next. Most houses Mary lived in had three rooms, bedroom, kitchen (small) and living room. The family moved frequently.

When asked to share her earliest memory, it was a story about living arrangements. **My youngest memory would be when I was about six because we lived with an older aunt, and I slept with her. She was old. I remember that. That sounds gross. And it was in two rooms. It was like a big bedroom and then a smaller room in the back that was both a kitchen and a bedroom because my mom slept in there. And there must have been three of us at the time. She (Mom) slept with all the little ones. And I slept with this old, old aunt. But I remember that because** for Christmas I got a pair of boots, brown boots with a buckle. (4th interview, March 7, 2023)

When my dad came home from overseas, we moved to live with a woman I called my Aunt Bebe and her husband who worked for the post office. They owned a duplex, and we lived on one side, and they lived on the other. It was two rooms and a bedroom and then a kitchen. Two huge bedrooms but the living room doubled as a bedroom, so we really didn't have a living room. I remember I slept in a crib till I was six years old because it was my bed. The boys all slept together—five boys.

When my aunt and uncle decided they wanted the house themselves we moved to a house with the same set up—living room, bedroom, and small kitchen. Sister Debbie and I slept in the living room on a pull-out couch. Mom and Dad slept in the bedroom when he was in town. And then all the boys slept in that third room which had a set of bunk beds and a full-size bed. All five slept there. A small kitchen. No yard. The backyard was concrete with a shed. The front yard was no bigger than this table because I used to cut the grass with scissors. We lived there until I was in junior high.

Then we moved over the bridge by the incinerator. We lived three blocks from it, and I remember that because my brothers would

throw stones at the rats on their way home at night. This house was like a duplex with a family in the front half and we were in the back. (4th interview, March 7, 2023). **I can remember being in high school and was an intense student; I liked to do my homework. I couldn't do anything until people left or went to bed because they were in my bedroom. Everybody lived like that.** (4th interview March 7, 2023)

What did Mary like to do as a kid? What did she read? Favorite foods? Did she get along with her siblings?

Four brothers and Mary. Behind Mary is a cousin.

We were outside all the time. I can remember playing cards. Plus, kick ball. Played baseball in the field and went swimming. We went to the pool all the time. In fact, I became the 9th grade swimming champ. But it helped to cool off.

Did your mom ever give you directions such as "Be careful when… or don't…. or be sure you…."? **No, my mom was so busy raising seven kids. I think she just assumed we would all take care of ourselves.**

We'd go to the movies which cost 25 cents in the neighborhood theater; it's still there. All the white kids sat on the bottom floor, and we'd throw popcorn over, just to mess with them. We'd have our feet up because the mice would be running along on the floor. One night we were walking home and Joe, of course, was on his bike and he was walking me home. Some guys surrounded us and tried to steal his bike. And I interfered and, you know, just pulled on Joe and said, 'Mom's waiting for us. We have to go home.' He yelled and screamed at me all the way home for making him look like a coward. He said he could take care of himself; he didn't need help from his little sister. (4th interview March 7, 2023)

When asked what her favorite book was growing up, she could not remember one. When asked if she went to the local library, she did not remember using it but remembered using the school libraries. Of course, she read textbooks because she liked school. Her one comment about not having a lot of books around the house growing up is **Maybe that is why I'm such an avid reader now.** And she is. She loves to get books at Goodwill, read them and take them back. She often has two grocery bags full of books ready to return and to get new ones.

Mary's father was a cook on the ships that were in and out of New Orleans. He was gone for many months at a time. But when he was home, he cooked. There would be a pot of food on the stove all the time. Red beans and rice were common foods. Jambalaya. Shrimp was cheap and was sold by travelling vendors who came through the neighborhood. The family never sat down and ate together because there was never a table big enough for all of them. And with the kids being busy, there was food available all day long.

My dad was not a trained chef, but he was a cook and he'd send these menus home and they'd be two pages long. He cooked when he was home, even more than my mom. Once he retired, he would cook something every day. He'd get up at 6:00 in the morning and the meal would be done by seven and it would be warm all day. When the mailman came, he would feed him; when the garbage man came, he'd feed him too. He'd make his own wine, keep it up in the attic and try to have everybody drink wine. My dad was very, very sociable in that

respect and he loved to feed people. He was quite a good baker. He'd make great cream puffs, but I don't think he did that as much in his later years. His specialties were the traditional jambalaya, gumbo, red beans and rice. Mom's specialty was spaghetti, red beans and rice which we ate almost three times a week. Seafood was cheap because a truck would come through the neighborhood selling three pounds for a dollar.

My brothers would fish. And it was always red beans, and you didn't have to cook it with any meat. Lots of rice. My dad had an actual rice cooker. He was one of the first people to have one because he traveled and brought back a rice pot from Japan. Nobody else had one. For breakfast we'd have coffee and crackers, sometimes cereal, but milk was expensive. My mom would make this powdered milk, which I hated. I'd have coffee and plain crackers crumbled into the coffee with lots of sugar maybe. You should try it sometime.

Lunch was at school. We'd bring our lunch because school lunch was expensive. We'd bring a bologna sandwich or what's called a sugar sandwich. Bread, with evaporated milk and sugar—butter was too expensive. Margarine maybe, but never butter.

We didn't have many fresh vegetables; they weren't very available. At one house we had a pecan tree. We had canned vegetables, canned peas, canned corn, canned green beans. That was it. Never had fresh spinach or fresh collard greens growing up.

When did you start eating fresh vegetables? **When I came here.** [to Minnesota] **I had my first asparagus. My first brussels sprouts too although I thought they were like eating baby cabbages. We might have had oranges once in a while at home. At one house we had a fig tree, which was great, but fresh fruit was expensive. We had canned peaches and canned pears.**

For dessert we might have had pecan pie, never sweet potato, or pumpkin pie. Once in a while my dad would make cream puffs. Mostly bread pudding for dessert because it was cheap—day old bread and milk. Bread was cheap. You could get that long po' boy bread. (4th interview, March 7, 2023)

Mary still cooks those comfort foods—jambalaya, bread pudding, red beans and rice, collard greens. In fact, two of her adult sons are in the restaurant business. One, Myles, is a regional manager of Applebee's Restaurants in the northern region of Minnesota. He learned the industry by working his way up, including beginning as a server. Mateo owns a restaurant named Krewe in St. Joseph, Minnesota. (A _krewe_ in New Orleans is a themed club that unites to celebrate Carnival.) Mateo's restaurant, Krewe, which specializes in foods hinting at southern flavors, has been given rave reviews in the New York Times, Minneapolis Star and Tribune and other publications. Many of Mary's recipes have inspired many menu items, including her fabulous bread pudding.

Food is still important to Mary as a way to build community. We will hear about this more when we talk about how she as a school administrator brings people together, and how she celebrates people and their lives.

Other than where one lives, what one likes to play, and what one likes to eat, it is fun to think about the earliest thing one remembers. Mary's early memory is a harbinger of many performances to come as demonstrated by the song she sang to become class president that was in Chapter One. **My favorite memory—hmmm. I remember in elementary school we had a variety show. I was part of a duo, a young boy and me. I was dressed up and he sang, "Let me Call you Sweetheart." He was on his knees singing "Let me call you sweetheart" to me. I smiled at him. That was one of the best memories.**

One famous person that made an impression on her and visited my school was Mary McLeod Bethune, a personal friend of Eleanor Roosevelt and the highest-ranking Black person in the federal government, when Franklin Roosevelt named her director of Negro Affairs of the National Youth Administration. **Another was when Eleanor Roosevelt herself came to our elementary school. We passed by her. She was in the hallway**

with our principal, and we all paraded in front of her. We saw Charles DeGaulle when he came to New Orleans. Our school was right on the driveway from the train station where he came from. And so, we all once again, stood on the sidewalk and waved as he went by. (4th interview, March 7, 2023).

Mary was raised in a Catholic family, like most of her neighbors. They went to church every week—at least the kids did. Her mom did not go, and her dad was rarely home. Mary later attended a Catholic university, Xavier. Even in a public elementary Mary's class would be escorted to church twice a week during the school day for religious instruction which was a common practice.

We all went to church. The kids all did. Yeah, we all did. Why? Because we have to go to catechism, you know? And now this was interesting. You'd like this. We remember we were in an all-Black school, Velena Jones. The district would release us either twice a week or once a week to go to catechism. So, we did. All the Catholic kids would leave school and they'd march us from Velena Jones to Corpus Christi, which was maybe, maybe a mile. And the teachers would walk us. (1st interview January 31, 2023)

Another crucial factor in growing up was education. This too was a harbinger of Mary's lifework, and it foreshadowed how and why Mary made such a difference in education in Minnesota, in particular, and nationally, as well. Although Mary's mom dropped out of school and her dad stopped attending in 3rd grade, education was important in the family, and it was expected that all the kids would graduate from high school. They continued from there to college, or technical college, sometimes taking advantage of a stint in the military to help pay for further education. Two brothers became welders which were in great demand because of the shipyards in New Orleans. One brother, Arthur, graduated from college as a lawyer and even became a politician in Louisiana.

Mary loved school and she loved learning. However, she took part in activities and the arts as well. In middle school Mary was part of a talent show and even oratorical contests. One year she performed "He's Got the Whole World in His Hands. Another time she recited this poem by Paul Laurence Dunbar:

Well, son, I'll tell you.
Life for me ain't been no crystal stair,
It's had tacks in it,
And splinters,
And boards torn up,
And places with no carpet on the floor—
Bare.
But all the time
I'se been a-climbin on,
And reachin' landin's,
And turnin'corners,
And sometimes goin' in the dark
Where there ain't been no light.
So, boy, don't you turn back.

Don't you set down on the steps.
'Cause you finds it's kinder hard.
Don't you fall now—
For I'se still goin,' honey,
I'se still climbin,'
And life for me ain't been no crystal stair. (Get it, 2022)

Every year when we filled out our little attendance sheet that asked what you wanted to be. I think in 7th grade I put down that I wanted to join the Army because that was what my brother just did. In 8th grade I said I wanted to be a phy.ed. teacher—why I don't know. In 9th grade my social studies teacher said, 'I think you should be a social studies teacher because, first, you're good at social studies and I think…You don't want to waste your brains being a phy. ed teacher.' I'll never forget this.

When asked who she admired, for Mary it was teachers, three, in particular, came to mind. One **was a fiery redhead—Leah McKenna, her** junior high principal. **Her husband was a college professor, and she was a dynamo. We had lots of activities at the school. We'd have our homeroom outside. She'd come out on the stairwell with her microphone and give us the message for the day.** (W-H dissertation, p. 36)

Another was Mr. White. He was an exceptional math teacher who inspired Mary to become active and join the math team. He also helped her get a scholarship to go to Xavier University. '**School was pretty much my life, you know, because there really wasn't a social life other than a little social club in high school.** (W-H dissertation, p. 41)

Third was Dr. Mack J. Spears, a Harvard Ph.D. graduate who chose to be a high school principal in a Black southern high school. **He could have left the South; he could have been a college professor anywhere, but he stayed until he retired.** (W-H dissertation, p. 41.)

He was a dignified leader who believed in the dignity of the profession, and its solemnity, but also in the responsibility and joy of being an educated person. Mary has continued his thoughtful legacy as she too believes that education is equal to freedom. She is relentless about quality and results for all children. (W-H, dissertation p. 105)

Dr. Spears created a model for how Mary would lead as a principal. She fostered and expected dignified behavior and dress. In fact, she would insist that students maintain appropriate dress and clothing. For example, **that's one of the cultural things that I hate to see--these kids braiding and doing hair in school or on the sidewalks. I tell them, 'No, this is not Central High School of Cosmetology." That is what people expect of a school with a majority of Black kids that you're going to be involved in activities that are really not appropriate for school. I said, "Comb your hair in the bathroom.'** The boys always have that little brush going.

'Use that in the bathroom, your hair is flying all over.' They know me; they see me coming and they stop.

'Well, I didn't do my hair this morning,' they'll say, 'Well, you know, you can't use that excuse when you go to work—sorry, take time to do your hair or at least make it presentable so you can come to school.' (W-H, dissertation, p. 113.) **'You are dressing for success here.'**

In her early academic career Mary attended segregated schools staffed by Black teachers and Black administrators. However, in Catholic college there were white nuns. At Valena C. Jones Elementary, Mary had to attend kindergarten twice because her June birthday allowed her to start one year early. When someone discovered her age, they refused to advance her and made her repeat kindergarten. The teachers were a strong, respected element of the Black community buying at the same grocery store and attending the same church. **Corpus Christi—it was a big, huge parish. Thousands and thousands—it's still there. It was an insulated kind of an environment because you really didn't know a lot about the Jim Crow world unless you ventured out. And of course, the older you got the more you ventured out. Then you got exposed.** (W-H dissertation, p. 35.

Not all school experiences were positive. Like most strong, negative emotional interactions, the feelings never go away. In 3rd grade **We had a** small cafeteria. If we brought lunch from home, we ate in our classroom. There were three Marys—Mary Long, Mary Smith, Mary Morrell—me. Mary Long, the clown, was running around the room and spilled the teacher's vase of flowers when she was out of the room. *This* Mary went up to sop it all up and of course, when the teacher came into the room, who did she see at her desk? That was me. It's so vivid, and I hope teachers don't do this—that woman picked me up and shook me in front of the whole class. I actually think I peed on myself. That memory, that abusive memory, is so vivid and that's why when you think about kids who are in abusive situations, they do remember. Those memories are very vivid; there must be a part of the brain that locks that in. Of course, she apologized but that memory—Mrs. Stevenson, I'll never forget her. She was a mean lady. That was my worst experience in school. (W-H dissertation, p. 34)

By grade six once more we see Mary demonstrating her ability to command an audience. She was recommended for gifted and talented programming because, ironically, of an original play she had written about the trials and tribulations of Biblical Job. She even published her own school newspaper which she created one page at a time. (W-H, p. 35)

Junior high was at Dr. Rivers Frederick Junior High which was within walking distance of home. It is where she began to think about becoming a teacher partly because of her principal, Leah McKenna. Music and being in a band are a strong cultural push in New Orleans. Mardi Gras, Second Line, Bourbon Street, and all the musical traditions and artists who have called New Orleans home really embrace the ability to play a musical instrument.

However, the family could not afford an instrument, so Mary did other things—sang in the choir (Maybe that is where she learned to sing her the song that led to her being class president), joined in choral readings, and participated in poetry readings. Plus, because she had utilized the public pool especially during the summer, she became an active swimmer and won City Champion in 9th grade. She was in student council and later ran for student council president. Again, we see Mary developing the varied interests and skills that make her the leader that she became. Her life is a living example of the need and power for children to experience a wide variety of opportunities, and exposure to many different chances to participate and excel. Sadly, we no longer have poetry reading, junior debate, choral readings which are participatory experiences that build confidence and self-esteem. But Mary knew personally the value of options, which is what she continued to insist upon and provide for the students at Central High School when she was the principal.

We had Black history in our schools. We had Black teachers who put it there. It wasn't part of the state's curriculum, but they always

infused it. We also had Bible studies. I had this one social studies teacher every day who insisted on starting class with students reciting a Bible verse. Each day the morning paper would have a Bible verse so I'd look in the morning paper where *The Times-Picayune* would have a Bible verse posted on the front page. . My brothers delivered papers, so I'd try to get the daily one down pat. I'd have to read the paper because I didn't read the Bible; Baptist kids read the Bible; Catholic kids didn't read the Bible. In her class if she called on you, you'd have to recite a Bible verse. But just in case I forgot, I'd fall back on the shortest Bible verse, "Jesus wept." That teacher, Miss Green—she was evil. If you didn't know a Bible verse, she would whack you with a stick on your hands. Of course, it was good because they would teach us Black history, but we'd also be infused with a lot of religion. (4th interview, March 7, 2023).

    The neighborhood high school was Clark, but Mary did not want to attend it because of its troubled reputation. Her junior high teachers encouraged her to apply for McDonough 35, a school for gifted Black students. It was the only four-year high school available to Black students until Booker T. Washington High School opened in 1942. (W-H dissertation, p. 38) Needless to say, she was accepted. She had to ride the bus across town to go downtown New Orleans on Rampart Street to get to school. She struggled to find 14 cents to ride the bus back and forth to school each day.

To earn extra money Mary would look for extra jobs. **I was a school lunch line monitor, making other kids stay in line and not jump the line. I would go last and get a free lunch if I were the line monitor.** (W-H dissertation, p. 40

These were the days before Rosa Parks. Buses were segregated. Black people had to sit behind the sign on the bus which designated which seats were for Colored people. **There were little bars on top of the seat; they had holes in them to hold the sign, and you'd have to move the sign. The sign** [for Colored Only] **could go up to the front if there were no whites. That's why when you see the iconic picture of Dick Gregory from the back of the bus, that's the last place that sign could be so the white people could never, ever sit on that long back seat. There was a sign, 'For Colored Only' right in back of that long, bumpy seat.** (W-H dissertation p. 32)

Dick Gregory was a Black comedian who authored a satirical book *From the Back of the Bus.* He even ran for President of the United States on the Peace and Freedom Party 40 years before Barack Obama was elected as the first Black American President of the United States

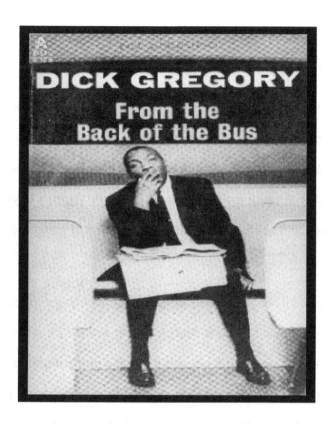

High School

     High school was the place that Mary began to use and develop the skills she had learned in elementary and junior high. It was a time of real growth, personally and politically. This was in the mid-1960s when the Civil Rights Movement was active with protests, speeches, organizations such as SNCC, Student Nonviolent Coordinating Committee, which promoted using peaceful, non-violent protests.   Most of her neighborhood friends went to the neighborhood Clark High School, but Mary got on the bus every day, crossing town to go to downtown New Orleans to a more rigorous, still segregated, school.

You didn't venture too much out of your own little community because you could get hurt. I think that's why I'm afraid of the police now. There was always a fear of the police, that they were ruthless and didn't follow rules. If you were Black, anything could happen to you. Even today when, if, I'm stopped by the police, I kind of shake—go into that old mode. (W-H, p. 42)

When asked if her parents helped guide her through these new and sometimes uncomfortable situations, Mary's response was, "**I was always different. My parents kind of left me alone. I really pretty much ran my own life—like a lot of kids do now. You pretty much make your own decisions and tell your friends what you're going to do. I never did anything bad, but they were not involved in terms of decisions.** (W-H dissertation, p. 41.

It was during high school that Mary ran for class president—and sang her song. She never shied away from other leadership opportunities. She became active in civil rights issues. As a junior, she joined the Negro Betterment Club, which was a group of Catholic students who wanted to integrate Catholic churches because churches were either all white or all Black. The way to protest in a non-violent manner was to have "kneel-ins" on

Sunday mornings. She and her friends would attend Mass in a white church and kneel quietly in the back row. This must have been frightening. **Imagine what it was like to have white parishioners verbally attacking you with vicious racial slurs. People would say awful things, but, luckily, there was never any physical atta**ck. (4th interview, March 7, 2023)

Joyfully, their group made a difference in for the integration of the Catholic church and church schools. The local Archbishop formally announced the end of segregation in the New Orleans parochial school system on March 27, 1962. Therefore, the school year 1962-63 was the first integrated school year in the history of the Archdiocese. Many Catholics were not happy. **I was still going to school in downtown New Orleans. It was chaos. I remember not being able to go home because the Catholic school board was located downtown near our school. There was a huge protest there and it spilled over to our school. Our school was surrounded by cars and people with bats so my administrators wouldn't let us go home unless our parents came and got us.** (W-H, p 44)

Mary was on the math team and Mr. White, one of Mary's influential teachers, was so helpful. **In junior high, I had had a great history teacher. I can't remember her name, but and then in high school, good teachers. Mr. White, I remember very fondly because he was my math teacher,** and I was on the math team. He was the one who kind of pushed me to go to Xavier. I mean, I wanted to go to college, but there was no money. And he got me a partial scholarship. And I think the summer before college, I was able to go to like a pre-college program there at Xavier. They invited a group of high school seniors to come to the university to experience what college was like. I got to know the school and campus. With the partial scholarship I received, it was very doable. My brother Joe, as crazy as he is, gave me the other $200 that I needed because it cost $400 a year. $400 plus $100 for student fees. My brother was in the Air Force, and so he sent me $20 a month. He was not married at the time so he could do this. Most of the historical Black colleges started the installment plans long ago and long before the white colleges, because they knew people did not have big chunks of money. I had the $200 and I paid the $20 every month and then luckily at the end of my first year, I got a full tuition scholarship for the next three years. And then I worked at schoolwork study, counting the Sunday collection. (1st interview, January 31, 2-23

Xavier University

Because of her talents and hard work Mary went to college, the first in her family. Xavier was the logical choice as it was a Black Catholic private university. The only other option for Mary would have been Dillard, a

Presbyterian college. At that time, the public universities were not very welcoming to a multiracial population.

In the past Louisiana received benefits from the Morrill Act of 1862 signed by Abraham Lincoln that granted federally controlled land to the states to establish institutions of higher learning, in particular, to meet the changing needs of the industrial nation at that time by featuring agriculture, science, military science, and engineering, as many other universities which focused on liberal arts. (Land grant universities, 2023) Because the South was still segregated, Louisiana established two land grant universities to keep the races apart. Louisiana State University (LSU) became a university for whites and Southern University was for Black students. **Mississippi, Alabama, Georgia did the same thing having dual land grant colleges.** (1st interview, January 31, 2023)

Like all seniors Mary had to take a college entrance exam even though the exam was given at the white Louisiana State University. **We got to take the test at Louisiana State University because the universities were newly integrated at that time. Mr. White, my math teacher—and a lot of teachers at McDonough had been Xavier graduates. At that point at least 50 to 60 percent of the teachers in the New Orleans public school system that were Black were Xavier graduates. Later, more graduated from Southern University and LSU but Xavier had the most for the longest time.** (W-H-p. 47)

When I started at Xavier, the nuns had banned all sororities and fraternities because there had been an incident in previous years behind where the university was located. Right now, it's I-10 but it used to be a canal. In a hazing ritual somebody was forced to try to swim across and drowned. So, the nuns banned the fraternities and sororities.

I did belong to a service organization. And we had our own Black honors society National Alpha Kappa Mu. (1st interview January 31, 2023)

At the end of her freshman year, she was awarded a full scholarship. Tuition worries were over. She also received the Outstanding Freshman Award. She had $675.00 per annum tuition paid for the next three years. But she continued working at the church and supervising the collection at Mass.

Mary was a day student. The only students who lived on campus were **from Texas, Alabama, and Florida—rarely northern cities. Usually, students came from other southern states from Catholic high schools. This was the Catholic college for Black kids in the South. If you lived in the city, everybody took the bus to get to campus.** (W-H, p. 48). She went home each night to sleep on the couch. Her mom was still caring for the four younger siblings and her father was still working on the ships and gone for months at a time. Mary went to a lot of places by herself. **My parents never—mostly my mom I would say, never stood in my way. I would**

just tell my mother what I was going to do, and she was OK with that.
(W-H, p. 51)

As a freshman she was inundated with the Catholic religion even though nearly half the students were Baptist. There was daily Mass at noon.

In her first year she was nominated Miss Freshman again campaigning. This time she had campaign flyers complete with a picture that was designed by brother Arthur who suggested the people "Vote for Mary Morrell." She won. In the South events honoring these winners were honored at formal events which required a nice gown for the elaborate evening and dance.

I thought, Oh, my God, why did I do this? Now my parents have to go through the expense which they didn't have—trying to buy all these things but I think the dress, if I remember correctly at that point only cost like $15. To buy the material and stuff. Somehow or another my mom came up with the money. Usually when I needed something like that, they'd come up with it. The men had to wear tuxedos and the women wore formal gowns. The young women were escorted by their professors and wore white flowing gowns with extravagant trains made from embroidered velvet. Mine was roses and luckily—we lived on Allen Street. Miss Fernandez made my dress out of tulle and made this beautiful train with red velvet. It had embroidered roses in it. The freshman queen was the Rose Queen and we each had

two attendants, then the Black Miss Xavier. **It was set up like a Mardi Gras Ball—you paraded in with your escort, sat on the throne and they had a big dance. That was the last time I ran for a homecoming competition in college. That was it.** (W-H dissertation, p. 49)

What did Mary major in? From the beginning she enrolled in teacher education and social studies coursework. (She obviously believed her teacher who told her she should be a social studies teacher.) Each year education majors had to be involved in student teaching. She taught catechism in an all-Black neighborhood at nearby Epiphany Church. Each of the four years she attended Xavier she taught the 7th grade boys' catechism class. (W-H, p 49)

Mary excelled in her classes with the exception of biology, which she nearly failed twice. She struggled with labs. **My physics teacher (at McDonough 35) was a graduate from Michigan State, but we didn't have any supplies. I remember our lab was just a regular classroom with a Bunsen burner. That's all we had. No tubes, nothing. So, when I went to college, I failed miserably at that—I aced the course --A's, A's,A's--- but failed the lab so I got a D. It was those labs that killed me. That was the last lab I took because I went into social studies education.** (W-H, p. 50)

This is another foreshadowing of why Mary Mackbee as a principal made certain that, one, there were high quality teachers in the sciences; two, that teachers of color taught those classes; three, that there were well-stocked science classrooms at Central; and four, that Black students were expected to be in science classes because they matter and they are "door-openers" to other jobs and education.

It seems like her junior years in high school and at university were crucial years. Sometimes kids in high school and teachers feel like the junior year is not as important as other years but, for Mary, her junior years brought new adventures.

In 1964 Mary went to the World's Fair in New York City while working at a Girl Scout Camp in upstate New York—by herself. She remembers buying a pearl ring. She had never been away from home and went "up north' to a huge city. She stayed with a family in Brooklyn and got lost once in the city but figured it out. (3rd interview, February 16, 2023)

During junior year in college, she attended a student leadership workshop in Madison, Wisconsin. She is not even sure how she got there, maybe by train to Chicago and then train or bus to Madison. In addition, she took a train trip to Washington D.C. These trips were all taken "up north," by herself where she was often a definite minority. Pretty adventurous!

Right after her junior year in college Mary met a priest from Selma, Alabama—remember this is 1965. In 1965 Martin Luther King and many, many others walked across the Edmund Pettus Bridge in Selma to make people aware of the need for a voting rights bill to protect Blacks from barriers which prevented them from voting. National Guard troops and the

Alabama National Guard were called out as Dr. King led 1000 marchers in prayer as they walked toward Montgomery, Alabama.

During this time a priest, Father Woulette, came to Xavier to recruit education majors to work in a summer HeadStart program in Selma. He brought Mary and three other Xavier students and a student from Boston University to Selma. Their white college chaplain, a friend of Father Woulette, drove the students to Selma, advising them that **when you go through these small towns, scrunch down. Even though he was a priest with a collar, he was driving two Black students to Selma to work there.** (W-H, p. 52) It could have been dangerous.

When in Selma, Mary and her classmates shared a house with a white married couple. **I did have visions of the Klan coming at night—you know, burning us down or dragging us off. In New Orleans you really don't see the Klan; they're not that prominent in terms of public exposure. But in Selma they were very public.** (W-H dissertation, p. 53

I was moved. Father Woulette gave such an impassioned speech about the needs of these kids in Selma. There were no jobs, and I was always looking for something to do. I really got subjected to dirt floors in homes in Selma. I didn't realize they'd pack that dirt down and it was hard as a rock. It's like a cement floor but it's dirt and it's glossy but you know it's dirt. Really poor kids—no shoes. (W-H, p. 53)

This Selma experience emphasized the skill that she used so often as a principle of not judging people based on where they live or what they wear.

Another key takeaway from Selma that would guide Mary in her future career is that Father Woulette gave Mary her own Missal. Inside the cover he wrote, "God gave you a great capacity to love; don't ever lose that." (W-H, p. 56) He recognized this great capacity of Mary's that became a cornerstone of her personality and her leadership style in later years.

During her college years Mary had another life-changing experience when she took a job as a camp counselor for the Girl Scouts in New York. Mary did not know anyone. She had never been to New York. She had never been a Girl Scout. She had never been to camp. She worked at this camp for nine weeks with twenty-five Jewish girls from the surrounding area.

Once I took a group on a hike, and we got lost. We were completely out of the reservation. We finally came upon a wooded area and spent the night; don't ask me why I did this—I'm sure there were bears digging in the garbage can next to us. The next morning, as we were walking, we came upon a beautiful house with a lake and a pool and, of course, we had walked completely outside the campgrounds. We got back on track—they didn't have to send a rescue party. (W-H-p., 59

Camp leaders were able to find humor in the situation and did not punish Mary. This job was foreign to her life experiences, but she learned. She had never stayed in tents before, never seen raccoons, or bats. She had seen roaches but never bats. In later years as Principal Mackbee she was always a willing chaperone on student council relationship-building experiences at a camp. Once again Mary grew from these experiences in that she was adventurous and courageous to try.

Mary graduated from Xavier with a major in education as a member of Gamma Kappa Mu, a Black honor society. She also received the Mother

Catherine Drexel Award as one of the top two students at Xavier. Mother Drexel was founder of the religious order and of the college.

So how did this woman with strong Southern roots end up in the frozen North? When she was a junior at Xavier, we see the beginnings of links to Minnesota. Xavier was part of an exchange program with St. Thomas University and Hamline University in St. Paul. Mary was one of four selected to participate. At the time St. Thomas was all male, so she probably would have gone to St. Catherine's. However, the four students found out that if they left the state and earned credits outside the state, the experience would not transfer back to certification in Louisiana. Consequently, they did not go. Instead, the professors came to Louisiana trying to hire more teachers of color. A deputy superintendent from St. Paul came with the professors and interviewed the three remaining students and hired all three of them, giving them what was called "pocket contracts" which meant they had a contract but did not know for what school, but that did not matter to them.

This was in 1966 when there was heavy desegregation in the public schools and a lot of white flight. For Black teachers in the South, jobs disappeared because when schools integrated, the white teachers went to Black schools, but the opposite was not true. Unfortunately, for the students most of the white teachers who came to Black schools were not as committed or of the same quality as the Black teachers who had been supplanted. Many of the Black teachers had graduated

from what they called normal schools but often lived in the community they served and were very dedicated to educating Black students even though they often had a two-year teaching degree. Those white teachers that replaced them were hired with four-year degrees so when Dr. Koch said, 'Come on up to St. Paul.' I did. Educationally, New Orleans was dying partly because the state had instituted the voucher system. A lot of white charter schools had sprung up. Most of the public schools are still Black including McDonough 35 where I went. (1st interview, January 31, 2023)

Alfreda, Lyn, and I came. Lyn left after a year and went to California. Alfreda and I had an apartment complex near where Sears used to be by the Capital [in St. Paul]. People told us that it was the ghetto. But I thought that this is like no ghetto I've ever known. I mean, in New Orleans, the ghettos are "ghetto." We had a couple who lived below us who had some friends with the Vikings football team. One day the neighbor told us the players were looking for Black women to take to a Christmas party because coaches were concerned about team members participating in interracial dating. We went. Fran Tarkington [former quarterback] **was there.** (1st interview, January 31, 2023) This was another happenstance which committed Mary to staying in Minnesota and set up many events that would affect her life, career, and family.

Another connection to Minnesota was, **I followed a boy.** She had been dating a boy who had earned a football scholarship to the University of Minnesota. In Louisiana he had gone to an all-boys' high school which was St. Augustine. Some friends got them together because both she and her friend were "brainy." They hardly dated but did go to prom together.

At one point she came to visit him, and the coach Murray Warmath was glad to see Mary's friend dating a Black girl. Warmath was a **good old Alabama boy and didn't like these Black players dating white girls. I fit the bill, although I didn't realize at the same time he had a white girlfriend the whole time he was here. I didn't know that until I came for his graduation next year.** (W-H, p. 60).

Eventually, Mary broke up with this friend and continued in Minnesota and was hired as a teacher aide for the summer. In the fall she was hired by Saint Paul Public Schools and began teaching grades seven and eight at Mounds Park Junior High. At that time St. Paul had passed a resolution pledging themselves to the goal of integrated education. Yet when Mary looked out at her classroom all she saw were white faces. Students were positive but parents were curious about her as a Black teacher.

Parents were more shocked at a Black teacher than the kids. Some of the parents were a little strange. Remember, I went to a Black school but many of the Black kids were as light skinned as the students at Mounds Park. I was used to a wide complexion of kids. I

remember one father at a parent conference, and he leaned over and said, "You have pretty teeth. I thought, 'Oh God, here we go.' (W-H, p. 64) That was one example of so-called "Minnesota Nice" which, as we will talk about more later, is often "Minnesota Passive-Aggressive." Mary said that the rules and expectations were clear in the South, but not as clear in Minnesota. Minnesotans were less comfortable talking about and living with racial differences so in an effort to appear welcoming, she was told she had "nice teeth."

In spite of being the only Black teacher on staff she felt she was approved of by staff and students. **No one questioned my ability. I don't know whether it was the air I gave off or the fact that they were welcoming."** (W-H, p. 64) Many of the staff were first year teachers and they worked hard, including Mary who taught English and Social Studies as a core course in a two-hour block.

It was a great system. We had one hour each day for conferences, either with kids, parents, or tutoring. Then we had one hour for prep [preparation], **so we shared all of our parent conferences during the day and conferenced with every student too. We only had 60 kids. The district eventually did away with this schedule because it was too expensive, but it was a great junior high approach.** (W-H, p. 65) However, subtle racist actions became apparent as time went on. More about this in the chapter on racism.

42

This was one of the varied approaches to scheduling and instruction that Mary experienced which gave her a wide background in effective scheduling and methods of reaching kids which she was able to draw upon as a district Director of Secondary Education and as principal.

In her second year at Mounds Park, she met her future husband Earsell Mackbee who was a Vikings football player. The head coach also did not want his Black players dating white women. By chance her neighbors invited Mary and her roommates to attend a Christmas party with the Vikings where she met Earsell. She agreed to accompany Earsell if he would come to her Christmas party at Mounds Park.

Of course, I was the most popular person because I brought a Vikings football player to our little Mounds Park Christmas party. He drove a Vette [Corvette] **so it was exciting. We didn't stay connected after that.** (W-H, -69)

Who was the Earsell Mackbee? He was born January 15, 1941, in Brookhaven, Mississippi. When they met, he was in his second season as a Viking. He had grown up in Vallejo, California, where he had entered the armed services right after high school. After his military duty, he attended Utah State University and played cornerback for their football team.

Later in the spring Mary and Earsell reconnected. She even went to California to meet his family. After dating for less than a year, they married.

I think I was buffaloed. He was divorced, so that was a no-no for me being a Catholic. I think I was just young. We were young, Catholic impressionable girls; we thought if we have sex with somebody, we had to marry them. I was young. He was only three years older than me but much worldlier. I think I was talked into that because somebody said, "Well, we heard Earsell on the radio saying, 'I'm marrying me a schoolteacher.'" (W-H, p.70.)

His so-called worldliness would become problematic as the years went by. They were married for 18 years, but those years were often difficult for Mary. There will be more on that in the chapter on Difficulties and Hurdles.

After three years at Mounds Park, Mary resigned. The commute from their home in Bloomington, the home Mary still owns, had been a hardship witnessed by the fact that Mary had five car accidents in that time. She wanted to work closer to home. Luckily, there was a long-term substitute position opening to fill a maternity leave in St. Louis Park. Mary was recruited by the Black school board chair as a candidate for this position. Just as in her first year at Mounds Park, when Mary looked out at her class, she saw just white faces looking back at her. There were only white faces in the teachers' lounge as well. **St. Louis Park was akin to my southern experience because it was very white at that point—I think I was the only Black teacher in the high school. A teacher who worked next door**

to me was from Jackson, Mississippi—white girl, who thought I was Arabic. I thought, that's because she can't write home to say she's teaching next to a Black person. Arabic—what's Arabic? I wasn't worldly. At that time, I thought, "What's Arabic" What a contrast to society by the time Mary retired. By that time, the US had been in several wars in countries where Arabic was the native tongue—Iraq, Iran, Afghanistan, Somalia and so on. Plus, Principal Mackbee at Central High School had a student population with many Somali immigrants to Minnesota. Understanding Islam, differences in food cultures such as understanding halal, and differences in clothing expectations particularly for women, had become commonplace.

Ironically, what Mary learned at St. Louis Park was that she did not like teaching senior high age students. Yet years later, she became a highly respected, well-known, successful principal of the oldest high school in Minnesota, St. Paul Central, for 25 years.

Mary wondered if the real issue was that these students in St. Louis Park were suburbanites when Mary had grown up in a major city and had then taught in another large city. This was a new experience. **The kids were very know-it-all. Really. There were some kids that said, 'You can't teach me anything.' I said, 'Well, then you can go to the library every day.' I don't think they'd ever had a Black teacher. I don't know if it's because I was Black or just because I was more of a junior high person**

–maybe I didn't appear intellectual enough. I did manage to survive the year. (W-H, p. 73)

She resigned from St. Louis Park; she and Earsell made the decision to start their family. Mary had not gotten pregnant in the early years of their marriage, so they decided to adopt. For some reason Earsell thought it would be great to adopt twins.

They were not able to adopt twins, but it came close. In 1970 they were selected to be parents to two boys. Mylo was only 11 days old; Myles Manning was two months old. Mary stayed home for four months, the first and only time she had not worked outside the home in her entire career. The boys and the instantly bigger family were a source of real joy and some difficulties. More on that in the chapters on Values, and Difficulties.

Mary needed to work because Earsell's earnings were not steady. At this point Mary called her Assistant Superintendent in St. Paul and asked if she could return. In 1971 she was assigned to Como Park Junior High. In 1975 Mary once again sought another professional growth opportunity. Saint Paul Public Schools had received a private grant to develop the Rockefeller Institute Program to identify, train, and support teachers of color to serve as school administrators. Again, Mary stood out and was chosen. In addition, another person chosen for the Institute was Nan Mizuhata, a woman who became a lifelong friend.

Nan was their surprise candidate because they were really looking for Blacks. Leave it to Nan—she applied, and they couldn't turn her down because she is a person of color; she's Japanese. That's when we met, and we've been lifelong friends ever since. That was a great year because we were interns. We got to travel and were paid tuition.

Dr. Neal Nickerson, Professor at the University of Minnesota, was supervising the program. Dr. Nickerson was one of the professors who went out of his way to recruit and support women to enter educational administration. He remained an ardent fan of Mary Mackbee and many other women in the state of Minnesota.

As part of the Institute, candidates were released from school one afternoon a week for seminars which were informational, and which helped develop a network that several women maintained for years. They were able to attend national conferences across the country to gain a broader perspective of educational administration. As a surprise, and to her delight, the grant did not require her to report the monthly stipend as income. This was particularly helpful as throughout most of Mary's married life she was the main breadwinner.

For our whole salary that year we didn't have to count as income because it was considered a fellowship. The experience literally

put me in the administrative role as an intern. We were on campus at the University of Minnesota one day a week. (W-H, p. 78)

Much to her surprise and dismay, shortly after joining the Institute, Mary discovered she was pregnant. She then learned that the Institute would be cancelled after two short years. It was an effective program and brought several women of color into administration. However, it was expensive and was cancelled. She finished the program just shy of the internship hours she needed to get her administrative license. The participants were going to be interns the next year at district expense. She was assigned as a teacher at Mounds Park Junior High. (W-H, p. 78)

Shortly after her return to teaching, she sought out the position of magnet school facilitator that could fulfill the need for internship hours.

Shortly after she completed her license, Mary was promoted to Assistant Principal at Harding High School. Once again, Mary was breaking down barriers for women and people of color. She **was the first female AP at a high school in St. Paul. Plus, she was the first pregnant woman assistant principal in St. Paul. Harding was tough—it was almost like Rice Street. Very blue collar. The kids drove fast cars and had beer-keggers every weekend somewhere.** Once again as in Mounds Park and St. Louis Park, staff wanted to know how she was going to perform. She was not only Black, but she was a female in a traditionally male role. **One**

Harding teacher said they were just going to sit back and wait to see if I could handle the job. (W-H, p. 79)

She must have been successful because Mary continued to get positions of leadership in the district.

The hierarchy of education was created by men. It was modeled after a military style of graduated levels of responsibility, with a person in authority with levels underneath of lesser authority. In the early days in the United States women could not even be teachers because their place was in the home. Eventually, they could be teachers but only of elementary age students because women were not seen as capable of handling older students. Plus, women could not teach if they were married or pregnant because they were supposed to be at home. Mary faced this underlying belief that women could not handle older kids. She proved them wrong.

To survive in the male-dominated role, which was more exaggerated when Mary began in the 1970s than it is even today, Mary utilized her contacts at the University of Minnesota, particularly Dr. Neal Nickerson and Wayne Jennings. The two men formed a group called *Women in Administration* which was designed to support women who wanted to become secondary principals.

We used to meet for encouraging talks. Neal was considered THE advocate for female administrative graduate students at the time. If you wanted to get your degree and needed to know how to maneuver

through the requirements, you got to see and wanted to see Neal. In the late 1970s there was a real surge of interest. Women began to see this as a possibility. We'd meet, we'd have formal meetings and speaker, and small groups talking about the problems for women in administration. Rosa Smith, [a one-time St. Paul teacher, high school principal in Minneapolis, and eventually Superintendent of Boston Public Schools,] authored a famous paper, "Women in Administration: Is the price too high?" because almost everybody [women] ended up divorced. We looked at 360 Colborne (the address of the District Administration Offices for St. Paul Public Schools) and of all the administrators down there, I think you could count on one hand the women who were still married. (W-H, p. 80). The inference is that the administrative jobs were hard on personal relationships. More on that from Mary's perspective in a later chapter.

Mary was Assistant Principal at Harding for four and a half years. It was a surprise to her when she was appointed principal at Jefferson Alternative-Career Study Center. I like to say they hired me over Curman Gaines; he was the obvious choice. [Why? Because he was male? Black?] It was between Curman and me and they picked me. Curman went to Hazel Park. (W-H, p. 81) Dr. Curman Gaines was eventually hired as Superintendent of St. Paul Public Schools and was Mary's boss. There were some difficulties between them in later years which will be discussed later as well in the chapter about Difficulties and Hurdles.

Her task was to create one large educational program from three, small, unique programs, to merge Street Academy, Out of School Youth, a program for special education students who had dropped out, and the Career Studies Program. What resulted was a unique one-stop-alternative school before Area Learning Centers were ever established.

She saw her task was to put integrity and rigor into the programs to create academic standards that would provide a valuable education for at risk students. She was there for 19 months. Considering her background that we have seen, this school was a perfect place for her to practice her belief in providing academic growth and rigor for all her students. Jefferson Alternative then became an excellent training ground for future administrators because it was a hands-on, integrated, rigorous program meeting the individual needs of at-risk individual students.

At that point if you were going to be an emerging principal, you did a stint at what was then the Career Studies Center. It was the toughest place—the APs (Assistant Principals) **were put there to see if they could handle the most difficult kids. At that time, they were not behavioral problems; most of these kids had attendance issues. Mostly dis-affected kids. They just didn't like big schools.** (W-H, p. 82)

As is true for many alternative programs, the previous reputation was poor. Sometimes people think that unless students are sitting in rows, quietly listening to a teacher, writing research papers, they are not learning. However, not everyone learns the same way, particularly those students who need an alternative option. Sometimes, educators included, think that because something is different, it is "dumbing down." Or an "easy A." When Mary came to Jefferson, students missing thirty credits were known to be able to graduate on time with a diploma. Mary did not tolerate a paper mill for a school. She has a quote, "Education is freedom." Everyone deserves to be free. Ergo, everyone deserves a good education. Her first step was to require a minimum number of attendance hours, a new grading system, and a legitimate work program. She had a budget of $40,000 which allowed her to pay students to work in real jobs, including day care centers and government positions. The pay was an incentive for students to stay in school. It also helped most of the students who needed the money. In addition to the twenty-five hours of schoolwork each week, students worked for one to two hours a day.

Her leadership style was a great fit because she became known for her ability to turn-around staff and students.

I don't know why they picked me because Curman had been AP at the Center and really had the experience with the kids there more than I did. Jim Phillips (Assistant Superintendent) **liked me; I know that I**

had worked for him as a teacher. Maybe they knew that Hazel Park was coming up and they wanted a man over there because that was a bigger school. (W-H, p. 82) This speaks to the sexist perspective. It also speaks to the fact that, perhaps, women administrators are more often put in charge of programs for students with special needs or even charter schools because they are thought to be more accommodating to differences.

She was at the Career Studies Center for the rest of that year and the following year. She was rewarded because of her success by being named principal of Harding High School. **In those days you didn't interview. The Superintendent just said, "Mary, we're moving you to Harding." And that was it.** (W-H, p. 82)

It can be a difficult transition to move from AP to Principal in the school where she had been the assistant previously. She was now THE leader. Yet to her advantage, she knew the staff and had a rapport with the teachers. It [the students and staff] **was very white. I'm trying to think if I had any teachers, maybe one or two, of color. It was pretty blue collar.** (W-H, p. 83)

This appointment was another example of Mary leading the way and breaking down barriers because this made her the first Black high school principal in Saint Paul Public Schools.
A high school principal, and Black too—we'd had Black elementary and middle school principals. At the end of the year several male teachers

came up to me and said that they had been watching me; they were giving a year to see if I was going to be successful—I passed their test. (W-H, p. 83) Mary could add Harding High School to the list of St. Louis Park Schools and Mounds Park where people told her they were just watching to see if she would succeed. Hooray for her! She did!

After three and a half years she earned another promotion, another one that she did not apply for or seek. In 1987 Mary was appointed as Interim Director of Secondary Teaching and Learning which was a position coveted by another colleague, previously mentioned as the woman who authored an article about women in leadership. **That's when I fell out with Rosa. In 1987 David Frey and Superintendent David Bennett were at the District Office. They called me down and asked if I would take the Interim Secondary Director's job.** David Frey had held the position but was being promoted to Assistant Superintendent. Mary had only been at Harding a short while. **I cried. I didn't want to leave Harding but they kind of twisted my arm. I didn't think I had a choice. They said we want you to come down as Interim Director.** (2nd interview, February 8, 2023)

She took the interim job for the remainder of the year and the job was posted as a vacancy in June. She had thought the position would be given to Rosa Smith, an aspiring Black administrator who had served in a district position as arts supervisor because Rosa had district level experience which Mary did not have at this time. The rationale for offering the job to

Mary instead of Rosa was that Rosa did not have the prerequisite experience of school principal. This decision at the district level caused some hard feelings between Rosa and Mary which will be discussed in the Hurdles chapter.

Later because of a demotion from this district position which will be discussed in the Challenges and Hurdles Chapter, Mary became Principal of Central High School, the oldest continuously operating high school in the state of Minnesota, a position she would hold for 25 years. **I thought. That's fine. I can go back to being a principal. It's a good job; it's one I love doing so it wasn't out of my bailiwick. My final act as Director was to appoint myself as principal of Central High School.**

At the time it was the only available opening for the 1993 school year. The current principal was taking a sabbatical to finish a degree and Mary needed a placement. **I said, I'll go to Central. I'll show him** [Curman Gaines]. **I'll take the toughest school in the district, and I'll show him I can handle it.** (Wilcox- Harris p. 96)

Enter Principal Mary Morrell Mackbee....

CHAPTER THREE
Central High School

It's important to understand Central High School in order to understand fully the vital role that school played in shaping Mary as an administrator and in perfecting her skills as a leader. As principal for 25 years, she became known as a dynamic, skilled administrator. She shaped the school, but the school also shaped her.

In 1847 Harriet Bishop is credited with having the first schoolhouse in St. Paul, the beginnings of the Saint Paul Public Schools, when Minnesota was still only a territory, not yet a state for another eleven years. In its beginning Minnesota was racially integrated in its many functions, hotels, schools etc. In fact, a teacher remarked that many students came to school wearing their blankets, suggesting that several students were Native American probably from Fort Snelling. In the early days there were more Native Americans in school than Black students. Ironically, it was not until 1849 when Minnesota achieved territorial status that some legislators decided to start limiting participation in civic matters to persons of color, such as disallowing jury duty or holding civil office or attending public schools. By 1856 still two years before statehood in 1858, Black children had to be educated in separate schools. But there had to be 30 students applying for instruction before the Secretary of the Board of Education would hire a separate teacher. This plan failed because teachers were hard to find, plus travelling to a distant school was a problem for students so enrollment dropped off. Between 1860 and 1869, the time of the Civil War and the 1865 Amendment freeing slaves, there was a migration of Blacks from the South to the state to Minnesota. Before other states even ratified the Fifteenth Amendment which was passed in 1869 and ratified in 1870 guaranteeing the right to vote, Minnesota passed a law guaranteeing all people the right to vote, being the only northern state to approve Black suffrage. In Democratic St. Paul, however, the largest city with the largest Black population in Minnesota, referendum voters solidly opposed granting suffrage to Blacks. But it was not until 1869 that a bill was passed that said districts in incorporated towns could not deny Black children admission because of their race if the schools wanted to receive state funds. (mnhs,2023).

Until 1866 there were no high schools in St. Paul. Older teenage students were taught alongside their younger peers in shared classrooms or shared buildings. (Onward Central, p. 5) The first high school known as "St. Paul High School" was established in 1866. (O.C, p. 6)

The school had 12 students and one teacher with a 38-week school year, divided into three terms. Classes were held from 8:30 in the morning until 1 o'clock in the afternoon, which is much like what European high schools do today. The curriculum was derived from classical studies, grammar, higher arithmetic, algebra, geometry, trigonometry, astronomy, universal history, physical geography, Latin, and geology. (O.C., p. 8)

In 1879 only 5% of the student population of St. Paul attended high school so when the then current building became too crowded, voters rejected the proposal to build a new school. However, by 1881 there were 200 students and the resolution passed.

The new building was a three-story brick structure completed in 1883. In the fall 223 students moved into the new 27 room schoolhouse, and the school was re-named "The St. Paul Central High." Six years later a 14-room annex was added to house laboratory space. Money was raised by the Debating Society to purchase an astronomical telescope, making the school the first in the state with a fixed telescope. (O.C. p. 10) Central was a leader in education from the beginning, which has continued.

Within a brief time, other offerings were added, including *The World*, a literary magazine, a debate club, yearbook, orchestra, and dramatic club. From its inception Central has been strong in supporting the arts.

By 1893, Mechanic Arts High School had its own building. Cleveland High School, which was renamed Johnson Senior High, was opened in 1894. Humboldt opened in 1889 as the first high school on the west side. (O.C. p. 13)

High school populations grew in St. Paul and across the nation as increasingly young people believed in the value of more learning. In 1910 only 19% of 15–18-year-olds were enrolled in high school and fewer than 10% graduated. By 1940, 73% of 15–18-year-olds were enrolled and 50% graduated. By 1955 the graduation rate was 80%.

Because the population had outgrown the building, the school district needed a new high school, preferably one centrally located. In 1910 they started building on the corner of Lexington and Marshall, which is the current location of Central High School. Some people wanted to name the school "Lexington," but alumni prevailed in their desire to keep "Central" as its name. Strong loyalty had developed to this school early on and has continued to this day. To recognize the street name of "Lexington," it was decided to make the mascot "The Minutemen" in honor of of the soldiers who fought at the Battle of Lexington in the American Revolution.

THE ST. PAUL CENTRAL HIGH SCHOOL

The new building, designed in "Collegiate Gothic," had three stories, a basement, and a sub-basement. It cost $419,154 and was designed to accommodate 1500 students. The first class graduated from here in 1912. In the beginning only 25% who started as freshman would go on to graduate. It was then decided to add manual training classes to the curriculum which "emphasized the intellectual and social development associated with the practical training of the hand and the eye" because most students expected that education would lead to a job. (O.C., p 17) Courses such as domestic science, woodwork, metal work, drawing and typing were part of the curriculum and, by 1925, the graduation rate was nearly 60%.

For the first time this new building had a dedicated lunchroom to "provide a brief respite from their tasks and an opportunity to get at a very small cost, a lunch of plain and wholesome food to supply new life and energy to their growing and developing bodies." (O. C. p. 19)

Through the design and construction process, three different principals served Central High School. By the fall of 1916 James E. Marshall took the position which he held for nearly three decades to become the longest-serving principal in Central's history. (O.C., p, 20) Mary Mackbee became the second longest to serve when she completed her 25th year. When one thinks about it, it is astonishing that in the 150-year history of St.

Paul Central High School, two principals were the leaders for 1/3 of the time--James Marshall and Mary Mackbee

By 1920 after WWI, most manual training schools had closed or become vocational and technical schools. With the rise of Hitler, there grew anti-German sentiment in a city where many could claim German heritage. Consequently, the study of German language and culture was discouraged, and some textbooks were banned. Plus, if a person was not a citizen of the U.S., they could not teach. (O.C., p 22)

One of the first Rhodes Scholarships (in 1902) went to a Central student--Henry Hinds. The scholarship offered a three-year course of study plus expenses. He was not the only Central student to receive such an honor. In fact, between 1902 and 1955 Central produced more Rhodes Scholas than any other public high school in the US; they produced a total of 11. From its inception Central has been known for its academic excellence.

Because enrollment continued to grow, by 1931 Central was changed to a three-year school and it remained so until 1944. During those years ninth graders attended junior highs.

In 1934 Central's enrollment was 2600 with 87 teachers, making a student-teacher ratio of 33 to 1. The national average was 24.9 to 1. By 1939 Central's graduating class had nearly 900 students.

Central was located on the edge of the Rondo neighborhood, a main center of St. Paul's Black cultural life. WWII was hard on everyone but particularly hard on the Black families. Most of the Black students attended Marshall High at this time until Marshall became a junior high and then they transferred to Central.

One Black student said, "When I went to Central High School in the fall of 1932 there were, oh, I would say, about 2,400 kids there. We were the boom kids from World War I. The largest number of Black students that was ever at Central in my four years I was there was thirty. Out of the eight Black kids that graduated in my class, five of them were on the honor roll." (O.C., p. 29-30)

Central has also been known for its athletic accomplishments. They were state tennis champions five times between 1930-1941. Many other teams did well. Women's basketball won the state title in 1976, 1979, 2007, and 2008.

In later years Central produced several Olympians over two decades. John Roethlisberger, a three-time Olympic gymnast graduated in 1988. Three-time cross-country ski champion and 1995 graduate participated in the 2002 Winter Olympics in Salt Lake, in the Luge event I believe. Micah Boyd was on the eight-shell team that won the bronze medal at the 2008 Olympics. He began rowing while at Central. Susie Scanlan, a 2008 graduate, won the bronze medal in fencing at the 2012 summer Olympic Games.

At one time Central even had a Rifle Club that had a practice range in the sub-basement of the school. It was rumored that there was even a bowling alley in the basement at one time.

Participation in sports increased in the 1920s and 30s and created the need for the new stadium named Griffin Stadium which was built in 1932 but was named in 1988, in honor of a1930s alumni, James "Jimmy" Griffin who would go on to become St. Paul's first African American Assistant Police Chief. The boys' track team used the stadium to prepare for their state championships in 1954, 1979, and 1989. The women were state track champions in 1977, 1978, and 1994.

The Black population was small throughout the1940s.

In 1954 the Supreme Court passed *Brown v. Board of Education* to put an end to segregated schools and the idea of separate but equal. St. Paul established a committee to look at racial imbalance in St. Paul schools. At the time there were 219 (9%) Black students four Native American, four Latino, and seven other minority groups at Central out of a population of 2,476 students.

By 1964 and the time of "white fight", the minority population of Central was 9%, with Black students as the largest percentage. By 1968, that number had risen to around 25%. Before the construction of Interstate 94 in the 1950s which destroyed the Rondo Neighborhood by running directly through the middle of this strong community, most Black students came to Central. Mechanic Arts was the only other choice. (O.C. p. 49)

During the 1960s there was unrest, protests, in almost every major city as racism was being confronted over and over. It happened in Central too.

Student activism by Central students helped bring attention to the broader issues involved in inequity in schools. Central students have always been active on the political front. Racism is something confronted on a regular basis.

By 1970 St. Paul would become a refuge for many Southeast Asian families. Hmong, Cambodians, Vietnamese, Laotians would make Minnesota, and particularly St. Paul, their home. Many Hmong students would come to Central.

By 1970 the overcrowding at Central would reach a crisis point.

In 1973 Central began the Quest Program, a program based on the Socratic method of discovery, and the first gifted and talented program approved by the Saint Paul Public Schools. (O.C., p. 55)

By 1973 there were 14 proposals for locations of where to build the new Central High School. It was decided to remodel the current building because its concrete 'bones' were still strong. To keep its status as the oldest continuously running high school in Minnesota, students stayed in the building during construction, taking classes in the morning and construction occurring the afternoon. Construction began in 1977 and was finished in 1979.

This new building had a completely different façade from the "Collegiate Gothic." One critic said it was "the nadir of modern school architecture in St. Paul, a building so resolutely grim and uninviting that it can only be viewed as a form of incarceration." (O.C., p. 60)

One of the pluses of the new building was an in-house swimming pool. Another offering was the new state-of-the-art "Black Box" theater which became such a strong program to give students another way to use their creative skills in dance and drama. It sponsored a Touring Theater that performed student-authored plays about contemporary issues schools throughout the state. Other schools tried to copy this program because it became so strong and helped many students stay engaged with academics.

Another addition was a state-of-the-art recording studio which was a real draw for many students to use musical interests in a way that may involve many facets of the industry, not just performing.

A graphic arts program allowed students to take Intro to Graphics, Beginning Screen Printing, and Advanced Screen Printing.

The music program with the bands, orchestras, choirs, and ensembles, including a Steel Drum Band supported the performing arts.

In the 1970s School Within a School (SWS) was another program to help struggling students stay in school and improve their basic skills.

In 1987 the International Baccalaureate program, an international approach to learning, originally designed to have a standardized program for expatriates around the world as parents were working in other countries, was introduced at Central. The program emphasizes areas of study in six areas: American and English literature, foreign languages, American and World History geometry, algebra/trigonometry, biology, chemistry, and electives such as art, Latin, music. One-third of Central students are in the IB program. If a student starts in the program in 9th grade and takes the required courses, passes rigorous tests at one or two levels, and authors a paper much like a capstone, plus, completing many community service hours, the student may have earned the equivalent of a freshman year in college by achieving the IB Diploma. IB is like the Advanced Placement program in that way, but AP does not require a proscribed program, capstone, or community service. Not every university accepts IB for college credit, nor do all accept AP. But the courses are worthwhile because they are intellectually challenging, rigorous, and invigorating.

It is rare that an urban high school is as successful with IB as Central. Central often had out-of-state visitors to see how they managed the program because within the IB parent organization, Central was recognized as a leader in its number of graduates and successful IB diplomas earned.

Remember Central for a long time was probably an ideal school in terms of poverty and race. We had it was 30, 30, 30,-- 30% white, 30%

Black, 30% Hispanic or Asian. And it was not economically the worst. You know, the poorest school, Washington probably was. And Humboldt on the West Side was largely Hispanic. Washington had a lot of Hmong kids at the time. But yeah, we were not the poorest school. But we were pretty balanced in terms of our ethnic diversity yet every time we got staffed, we were considered a low poverty school, actually.

(5th interview, March 21, 2023)

In 1994 Central began offering Advanced Placement Courses for students to earn college credit while in high school. Central also offered College in the Schools, a partnership with the University of Minnesota for students to earn college credit while in high school. All three programs, IB, AP, And CIS, require specialized training for teachers.

Minnesota also has PSEO, Post Secondary Enrollment Options, where students in 10th, 11th, and 12th grades, if they have a B average, can leave the home high school, go to a college campus, and take a college course that is paid for by the state, including textbooks.

In 1968 in recognition that to fulfill the recognition that not all students are going college-bound, Central purchased a garage at Selby and Dunlap near the high school to use for a hands-on auto mechanics course so students did not have to leave Central to go to a technical college, they could just walk one block and take this wonderful course that helped many students stayed engaged in school, plus they fixed many cars.

A recent addition is AVID, a program to help students, particularly newcomers to our country, who have never had a family member go to college. It is designed to get students ready for college by knowing how to navigate the system and be prepared academically.

Over the years Central's graduation rate has been over 90%, which is often attributed to the fact that there is a plethora of options for all types and kinds of learning. In addition, they do not just graduate, but many graduate with honors whether with an IB diploma, AP courses, as a National Merit Scholars, or Semi-Finalists. About 77% of Central students attend some form of post-secondary education. (O.C. p. 74)

This is a wonderful reputation. No wonder Central earned, and was rewarded, by being named as a National Blue Ribbon School of Excellence in 1997-98. Few urban high schools achieve that recognition. Mary Mackbee played a significant role in this achievement in this school, along with the marvelous students, of course, teachers, parents, and community members. A school who earned this national award was then allowed to hang a banner outside of the school for five years that publicly recognized this achievement to let the neighborhood know of, and join in, the pride of this accomplishment.

It is impossible to list all the graduates of Central who have gone on to make a difference. There are judges, lawyers, police chiefs, mothers, fathers, even the current mayor of St. Paul, Melvin Carter, are Central graduates. Alumni continue to come back to support the programs and provide scholarships because Central mattered to them. It strikes a chord in the hearts of anyone who attends.

The changing demographics contribute to Central's success and its hard work. In the 1980s the influx of immigrants from Southeast Asia altered the demographics of Central. Recently, immigrants from Africa have settled in St. Paul, including those from Somalia and Ethiopia, Liberia, and Nigeria. Minnesota has the ninth largest African community in the country. The Central Minority Education Program (CMEP) formed in the early 90s has grown to meet some of these diverse needs. O.C., p. 76)

In the early 1990s Central has provided a supportive environment to a group who called themselves the GiBLeTs, Gay Lesbian Bisexual Transgender.

Plus, during Mary's tenure she brought in a construction academy and teacher preparation academy to try to help students, particularly students of color, get a taste and begin the preparation for careers that need them.

Overall, the depth and breadth of the programming and support for students at Central is unparalleled. Graduation rate of 91% is higher than the national average of 82%. IB and AP courses continue to provide rigorous academics.

Diversity is another of Central's assets and identity. Today, the students of color make-up about 2/3 of the population. (Someone said the minority population is 2/3 but that is not a minority, it is a majority.) Thirty-nine languages are spoken in the homes of Central students, and many are first- and second-generation immigrants.

Economically, Central has a wide range. In 2016 49% of Central students received Free and Reduced Lunch.

Mary Mackbee has been a cornerstone of the transition of the education system of the 60s and 70s to meet the changing needs of our populations of the current times by providing a wide range of offerings and support. She has made sure there is a welcoming atmosphere in the school. The school is not stuck in the past, nor does it rest on past accomplishments; it continues to change and respond, yet keeping the traditions and integrity of what has become the Central High School ethos by continually looking forward.

When taking the job as head principal of Central High School Mary felt her job was to bring the school back to the community to be highly respected. **It had been highly respected and one of the best high schools. When I went there in '93, they had the IB program which had begun a couple of years earlier. So that was growing. However, the community didn't see that as a program for Black kids. They saw it as a program to attract white kids to Central. And it did. We had students** from Stillwater, Roseville. We had Black kids from Roseville always. I felt the environment was a little stifled, but I just hoped to bring it back to its prominence like it was in the '50s. You talk to graduates and there is such loyalty and pride in that school. (1st interview, January 31, 2023)

To get an inkling of some of the graduates of Minnesota' oldest high school in continuous existence, just look at the list on Wikipedia of notable graduates, which does not even include all the local notables:

- Neal R. Amundson, head of the University of Minnesota's chemical engineering department, 1949-1974; known as the "father of modern chemical engineering."
- Martin Apple (1956), molecular biologist and president of the Council of Scientific Society Presidents
- Jeanne Arth, former U.S Open Doubles champion and Wimbledon Doubles champion[35]
- Rita Bell, singer and actress[36]
- Micah Boyd, 2008 Summer Olympics crew rower[37]
- Melvin Carter, current mayor of Saint Paul[38]
- Joshua Cain, co-founder and lead guitarist of American pop punk band Motion City Soundtrack
- Elijah Campbell, American football player.
- Midge Decter, editor and author[39]
- Thomas M. Disch, science fiction writer and poet[40]
- John Drew, Minnesota state legislator and businessman[41]
- Colton Dunn, actor and comedian[42]
- Amelia Earhart, aviation pioneer and women's rights advocate, attended briefly before moving to Chicago[39][43]
- Dave Frishberg, jazz musician and author of "I'm Just a Bill"[44]
- Michael J. George, Minnesota state legislator[45]
- Leigh Kamman, jazz musician and radio host[46]
- Jawed Karim, co-founder of YouTube[47]
- Jeff Loots, gridiron football player

- Harvey Mackay, Chairman of MacKay Mitchell Envelope and New York Times Best Selling Author of Swim With The Sharks[48]
- Joe Mande, actor and comedian[49]
- E.D.I. Mean, born Malcolm Greenidge, member of rap group Outlawz[50]
- Frederick Joseph Miller, Minnesota state senator and lawyer[51]
- Gordon Parks, photographer, filmmaker, and writer.[52]
- Stacy Robinson, National Football League wide receiver with the New York Giants who has two Super Bowl championships.
- John Roethlisberger, three time Olympic gymnast[53]
- Dua Saleh, poet and rapper[54][55]
- T. Denny Sanford (grad. 1954), banker and ranked #117 on Forbes list of richest Americans[56]
- Charlie Sanders, actor and comedian
- Susie Scanlan, bronze-medal winning fencer at the 2012 Olympics.
- Charles M. Schulz, author of the *Peanuts* comic strip[57]
- Richard M. Schulze, founder of Best Buy[58]
- Max Shulman, a 20th-century American writer and humorist best known for his television and short story character Dobie Gillis[citation needed]
- Don Simensen, American football player
- DJ Skee, DJ, radio personality, producer, and television host
- Danez Smith, poet[59]
- Nick Swardson, actor and stand-up comedian[60]
- Jon Wiener, historian and political commentator[61]
- Stokley Williams, American singer, record producer, and percussionist[62]
- Dave Winfield, Baseball Hall of Fame left fielder[35]\ (Wikipedia, 2023)

Although Mary Mackbee did not graduate from Central High School, many consider her a notable of the school. If one listened to the speeches given at her retirement, her leadership and love of the school were apparent. Her goal of bringing the school back to the community with the respect it had in the early 50s and 60s was accomplished that. In addition, she has kept it primed for the future.

A student Booth McGowan says, "To be a student at Central High School is to be a part of something terrific. Something that is composed of friendship, love, community, and a fair share of the real world. There is so much talent, knowledge, and life experience in the student body. It is incredible." (O.C. p. 81)

CHAPTER FOUR
Firsts, Awards, Accomplishments

Part of this memoir is to recognize the accomplishments and leadership of Mary Morrell Mackbee which are an outgrowth of her life experiences. This is part of the apeirogon that cannot be separated.

Mary Mackbee has been a person who has broken, or tried to break, barriers and practices that do not make sense, either in the past or now. She has done things quietly without expecting or wanting any fanfare. However, anyone who knows her, or who gets to know much about her, will suddenly realize the depth and breadth of what she has done.

Just the fact that Mary was raised in the segregated South and made a home in the white, frozen North and became a leader in a field dominated by white males is an accomplishment all by themselves. But there is a lot more....

If an accomplishment, a first, or an award has been omitted, this author apologizes it is impossible to get a complete list, depending on who one talks to. They are cited in no particular order because it is hard to prioritize any one deed as more important than another because they all are significant. One cannot even organize them by time achieved because they are so intertwined.

Here goes:

Breaking Barriers—Firsts

First Black principal of a St. Paul high school

First pregnant female Assistant Principal in St. Paul—at one time, if a woman becamepregnant, she had to take a leave or resign.

Part of a group called the Negro Betterment Club who conducted a "kneel-in" to integrate Catholic churches in New Orleans.

> The young women knelt quietly in the back of the church and were spat on, called names, and ridiculed.

First to go to college in her family

First Black principal to be named Minnesota Principal of the Year

First St. Paul employee to negotiate the use of sick leave to be used as maternity leave. Prior

> to this, women had to take a leave of absence, so would not be paid.

First St. Paul principal to design a one-stop multi-service center for an alternative high school. before Alternative Learning Centers were developed

First female to challenge pay disparity for administrative positions in St. Paul between the salary a man received and what she received. She won.

First who exited a position at District Office to assign herself as a high school principal.A position she held for 25 years, turning a Demotion into a PROmotion.

First St. Paul high school principal to create an all-female administrative team of only female principal and assistants.

Awards

City swimming champion in 9th grade in New Orleans

High school class president

A scholarship to Xavier College because of academics

- One of top two in her graduating class from Xavier
- Won acceptance to McDonough 35, a high school particularly for Gifted/Talented Black students because of her academic record and leadership
- On math team in high school for gifted math students
- Member of Alpha Kappa Mu, a national Service Society
- Chosen as one of four students to be part exchange program between Hamline and St. Thomas University and Xavier students while in college
- Miss Freshman at Xavier University
- Member of Gamma Kappa Mu, a national service sorority
- Received the Mother Catherine Drexel Award for being one of the top two students at Xavier
- Chosen to be part of Rockefeller Institute Program to identify, train, and support teachers of color to serve as school administrators with University of Minnesota
- 1987 Administrator of the Year from St. Paul Counselors Association
- President of St, Paul Public Schools' Principals' Association
- Charter participant in Bush Principals' Leadership Program
- 1988 received Spurgeon Award
- 1988 Minnesota Association of Secondary School Principals' Capital Division Principal Of the Year
- 1996 again Minnesota Association of Secondary School Principals Capital Division Principal of the Year
- 2000 Liberty Bell Award from Ramsey County Bar Association for her contributions to Law Day Seminars
- 2000 Big Brothers Board Award for her service to Big Brothers organization
- 2001 Community Service Award nominated by a parent.
- Board member of North Central Regional Board

2007 Century College's Woman of Distinction

2008 International Baccalaureate Inspiration Award from International Baccalaureate Board

T.A.S.K. Award from Central High School Assistant Principals

2009 Herbie Award, named after U.S. Hockey Coach, Herb Brooks

Chair of State Board of School Administrators for twelve years

Upon her retirement, St. Paul Central Auditorium named for her.

These awards do not account for all the daily thank yous and kind thoughts for all the good things Mary did for people. If you think about it, in the 25 years at just St. Paul Central, Mary was a role model and influence in the lives of around 52,000 students, their parents, the staff, and community. She practiced the idea of "pay if forward," to do something kind for someone with the hope that they in turn will do something kind for another. Mary constantly did that with small gifts, acts of support and kindness, food, flowers, parties, the list goes on. Thank you, Mary.

CHAPTER FIVE
Challenges and Hurdles

It is easy to call Mary "resilient." Books are written about resiliency as a skill necessary to help deal with our rapidly changing world. School districts have used the idea of promoting and encouraging resiliency even with students, recognizing it as a valuable life skill. But what is it? Here is Mary's definition, **"Did anybody die? If the worse that could happen, did not happen, then we can deal with it."** (2nd interview February 8, 2023) Others define _resilience_ as the ability to keep moving in the face of difficulty. It is the ability to bounce back into shape, like a rubber band. Mary has had many opportunities to practice bouncing back. What amazes this author is that, not only does she bounce back, but she does so without bitterness or anger. What challenges and hurdles did she face that taught her resiliency?

Poverty

In Chapter Two we learned about Mary's growing up in New Orleans. In a family of seven kids and a father whose job took him out to sea for months every year, it was not easy. For Mary's mom, Mimi, who was busy raising the children alone for most of the year, = it impossible to even think of getting a job outside the home. Mimi had worked as a domestic worker before she married but was not able to continue after the babies were born. Plus, in their neighborhood in the Seventh Ward, jobs, especially those with a living wage, were not easy to come by. Mary's mom did not drive, and they did not have a car, so transportation was an issue.

Sometimes feeling poor is defined by the company one keeps. For example, if one lives below the poverty line, and everyone in your circle of friends is in the same situation, then one does not feel as disadvantaged as if you were living below the poverty line and you were surrounded by people who were wealthy. Although Mary's family was poor, so were her neighbors mostly. Although some of her neighbors were teachers, businessmen and one of her neighbors was a lawyer and had a nicer house, they all lived together in Seventh Ward because it was the segregated South.

New Orleans is known for its shotgun houses. Living situations were crowded, with the family as it grew crowded into three room shot-gun houses. No hallways. Living room, bedroom, small kitchen. Mary often slept in the living room, which meant that if she was going to study, she had to wait until everyone was sleeping. As a young child until she was six, she slept in a crib because it was a way to create another sleeping space. Otherwise, the boys, anywhere from three to five of them, had to share a room; Mary and sister Debbie shared the pull-out couch. The girls had it a little easier in some ways.

Meals were "on the fly," so to speak. Food may be cooking all day—a pot of beans and rice, for example, but because the kitchen was tiny, there was never an opportunity for the entire family to sit together around a table for a meal. The kitchen was not big enough to hold a table that size.

Plus, the houses were often shared duplexes, or the rooms were shared with relatives. Mary's parents did not own a house until Mary was an adult. But everyone lived that way; it was not unusual.

Therefore, the kids were outside much of the time, which was not a bad thing. They had to learn to play together, take care of one another, learn to get along and resolve differences. Entertainment had to be cheap. Kids were not driven to scheduled activities, classes, or sports or play dates as kids expect today. That also is not a bad thing. Entertainment also had to be cheap. They used the public pool—segregated, of course. It helped cool off in the hot Louisiana summers and helped Mary develop into the city swimming champion in 9th grade. They also played such games as kickball or kick the can.

They went to the movies for a quarter —segregated again with the Black kids in the balcony. The movies were serials which means that the movie would end with a cliffhanger, prompting the viewers to return for the next installment. Now we "binge" on serials as they are broadcast on Netflix or Amazon Prime. They watched Lash LaRue, an old-time Western movie star who had been born in New Orleans. His movies had "chapters" to encourage viewers to keep coming. They would show one movie and leave it with an unfinished ending so one would come back for the next segment.

There were not a lot of books in the house. Mary does not remember using the library in the neighborhood; she was not sure if there was one. She used the school libraries.

There was always food—simple, but always there. Red beans and rice, jambalaya, shrimp, bread pudding, po boys, sugar sandwiches, and so on. The neighborhood grocery store in walking distance was a small local store owned by an Italian who did not live in the neighborhood.

The options were limited by the size of kitchens, refrigerators, etc. The grocery stores did not carry "exotic" foods. As she told us, the first time she had brussels sprouts, for example, was when she came to Minnesota. But again, this situation of the lack of fresh vegetables in small neighborhood markets was more common at that time. Megastores were yet to be developed. The kids mostly brought their lunch to school because purchased school lunch was expensive and there were seven of them. They had "sugar" or bologna sandwiches, most likely.

They were frugal with clothing. People sewed and repaired tears, let out hems, etc. One of the stories Mary told us about clothing was when she needed a gown when she was Miss Freshman. Luckily, her mom found the money for the material and a neighbor was a seamstress and made it for $15.00 but because of the expense, which was considered an extra, she never ran for any position again that required expensive dress and might cause a hardship on the family.

School cost money too. But there was an expectation that all her family would graduate from high school even though neither of her parents had done so. Maybe that's why it was so important. Plus, due to scholarships and the G.I. Bill, all the men got further training as adult through technical college or the military. Education mattered. Education was freedom.

In high school Mary had to take the city bus—14 cents each way. She worked to earn some money for that because with seven kids to raise, money was tight. She knew she wanted to go to college but was worried about the tuition money. As stated earlier, she earned a scholarship, paid on the installment plan with $20 a month with the help of her brother Joe, and then earned a full scholarship. Of course, she lived at home because living on campus was not economically feasible.

Mary was resourceful in that she took odd jobs to earn some money. She was the line monitor in high school, ironed clothes for her cousins, and did some minor housework. Everything helped.

When asked about the effects of poverty today when people say that generational poverty is a major factor in the achievement gap, Mary has a different take. She does not let anyone off the hook because of poverty. She grew up where everyone was poor. **You had to survive, usually in intergenerational homes, everybody living together. We did it. You have to work at it and want it.** Mary and her family prospered; they did not feel sorry for themselves; they had goals and worked to achieve them. Her whole family exhibited resiliency.

Sexism

Years ago, Shirley Anita St. Hill Chisholm was the first Black woman in Congress (1968), the second female to be elected to Congress from New York, and the first woman and in 1972 the first Black woman to seek the nomination for President of the United States from the Democratic party. Her campaign was a bid to be nominated instead of the Party giving it to George McGovern. Earlier in 1964, Margaret Chase Smith had been the first woman to run for President, but she ran for the Republican Party. One of Chisholm's famous quotes is "I had met far more discrimination because I am a woman than because I am Black." (Quote fancy, 2023) She also predicted that a Black man would be elected President long before a woman. She was right. Obama was elected in 2008, 36 years after Shirley Chisholm ran—a generation apart. We still have not elected a woman to be President of the United States.

What was Mary's experience as a woman? On one hand she was raised in a family with five brothers and one sister, which, in a way, was an asset because she learned about men daily. Plus, because her mother was the main parental resource to the kids as her dad was onboard ships for many months a year for his job, she learned that women need to be able to cope. Women must be strong in their own right.

As a secondary teacher Mary entered a male-dominated profession. As an administrator, that was even more pronounced. She became first pregnant high school assistant principal in St. Paul and the first Black head high school principal in St. Paul. Plus, as a female she broke some barriers when she demanded the use of contractual sick leave to be used for maternity leave which had not happened before. Prior to Mary, women had to take an unpaid leave.

Over the years in her roles as assistant principal and head principal, she was told at least three times that teachers waited to see if she as a woman could handle it, meaning could she handle high school students and the typical male role of head high school principal. She proved over and over that she could.

At the district level when she was hired as Director of Secondary Teaching and Learning, there was a man hired as Director of Elementary Teaching and Learning which was unusual because elementary education is often thought of as a female domain. It may have been to have a balance of male and female, but it does not always happen.

Sexism was vocal when rumors circulated that Mary and her colleague were having an affair, because she and her male colleague, worked closely together. They were the only two in those positions in the district. People find it difficult to believe that men and women can be good friends, work closely together, but not be involved sexually. **I think people**

didn't understand, and they still have problems with colleagues who are equals, being male and female, having a friend relationship rather than it being sexual. I think people still have problems with that in terms of seeing people. Some of my best friends have always been males. Maybe that was part of the culture; at that time, the belief that the only way you got to the top was to sleep your way through. (W-H, p. 87)

Her work with her colleague precipitated another first. Mary found out that he was paid more for the same job. **I was mad. Well, definitely it was a gender thing. It was more of a gender thing because here was a man being promoted after me and getting put on a higher pay scale.** (W-H, p. 87) Hence, she wrote Superintendent Curman Gaines a letter.

'According to our contract, we can appeal our salary placement to the superintendent if we feel that it's unjust. I have been in the position longer; I have the same level of experience, yet he was placed at a higher level. I think this is a cause for a discrimination suit. My remedy would be that I would be place on the same level as he is currently back to when I was originally appointed in April." Curman said, "Fine." He did it. (W-H, p. 88) Again, Mary challenged the status quo and won a victory for human rights and women's rights.

I knew Curman and I knew he would be fair—at least at that time I thought he would be fair. I really didn't think it would come back to

haunt me. I was right—and that's why I wrote it because it was the right thing to do. It was an injustice at that point of have my colleague being appointed after me in October and be put on two—two steps ahead of me. (W-H, p. 88)

Sexism is played out in other ways such as expectations of how one dresses, one's hair styles, use of things such as nail polish. How one dresses and acts can either stimulate that type of talk or help downplay it. Consequently, Mary chose to dress conservatively to minimize comments about her appearance. **When I was first in administration, I always wore pant suits. I see myself as traditional in style, hair…fabrics.** (W-H, p. 87) For example, Mary and her female assistant principal decided to make things easier and almost standard. Her assistant **and I decided suits are really cumbersome. We went to vests. We would alternate our 'uniform.' We would wear black pants, black vests, and a red shirt** [Central school colors], **or we would wear black pants, red vest, and a black shirt and alternate. That became our uniform. In fact, when I substitute in schools now, I still wear vests just to get away from the suits. I don't know when I've worn a dress—maybe weddings, but I'm a pants person because it's hard to be so physically active in dresses and heels. I stopped wearing heels when I went to Central because there was so much walking. Plus, I needed comfort shoes on those terrazzo floors.** (2nd interview, February 8, 2023)

In conversations with women aspiring to educational leadership roles, there is almost always conversations about dress, hair, and fingernails. Some trainers even advise avoiding bright colors, ruffled blouses, or elaborate, colorful fingernails. For Black women there is a discussion about hairstyles, braids or no, curly, or not. Gradually, some women are claiming the right to dress as they choose and have natural hairstyles, but if one looks at powerful women such as those in Congress, one will see them in pants suits and conservative colors. If one remembers the presidential campaign with Hillary Clinton, one will remember the constant conversation criticizing her pants suits and hair styles. Minnesota's own two women state senators are seldom photographed in clothes that are not dark colored pants suits. Nancy Pelosi, former Speaker of the House, does not always follow that as she wears dresses, colorful ones, and high heels. But maybe her longevity and respect helped her carry it off.

In the predominantly male environment, the women administrators of St. Paul formed groups designed to support one another which is something we all need, whether male or female. One such group was a group called Women in Administration which was led by Dr. Neal Nickerson from the University of Minnesota and Wayne Jennings. Women would meet periodically to talk about issues they were experiencing, and then problem solve them. This group was mostly women from St. Paul. **We could commiserate about the clueless men that we had to deal with and then** just support each other. People would call each other if they had problems. When I went to the District Office, I got involved in this strong and beautiful women's group made up of district administrators.

Apart from the group sometimes some of us in St. Paul would meet periodically for lunch. There were about nine of us. We called ourselves Strong and Beautiful Women. One had a cabin in Wisconsin, and we would go there twice a year—once in the summer and once in the winter for a retreat weekend. We went to relax but we talked shop a little bit. But mostly it was to have a bond, a support group. We'd talk shop, complain, and congratulate each other. We needed it. Some people were having family issues, so they were able to get support there.

When asked if the men in district something similar, her comment was **They golf and they played poker. I don't think they retreat and let go and share family or work issues. They go golfing or fishing. For example, when I was at Harding the guys all had a fishing retreat every spring. I wasn't that interested. I don't even fish. One of the female teachers wanted to go on one of their trips. She told me she didn't want to go by herself, so I said I'd go with her. I thought I'd support her. We had to put down 20 bucks or something like that so we both signed up.**

About two weeks later, we got all our money back. The trip was cancelled. The wives had revolted. Then the men cancelled the trip.

Technically, the reason was that it was one big cabin where everyone stayed. There was really no privacy, so they were trying to figure out how to accommodate us in this all male bastion. They cancelled. I was glad because I really did not want to go. (4th interview, March 7, 2023)

Even in retirement Mary continued to have strong connections with some of this group.

This author completed a study of women head high school principals in school year 1994-95 to ascertain their "Key Determinants of Success." In this study the women

felt they were successful because they thought of themselves as women first and principals second (Sigford). So did Mary (She was one of the members of that study.) **I guess I'm maybe a woman first because I think my response to staff was as a grandmother or a mother or a wife in looking at issues. If you look at the tasks of management and decisions as the major task of a principal, I was more oriented to a relationship-oriented approach. So, I guess as a woman first.** (3rd interview, February 16, 2023)

The discussion among women administrators is often whether one must lead like men have done or if one can develop and use one's own style. These women would say that it is important to lead who they are, not lead like someone else.

Racism

In spite of Amendments to the Constitution, the Civil Rights Movement, and constant training in business and industry, politically, we are currently faced with a polarized country with more hate crimes, including racially biased ones, than ever. Nationally, reported hate crime incidents increased 11.6% — from 8,210 in 2020 to 9,065 in 2021. (Justice, 2021) We hear every day where someone wants to change what is taught in high school to eliminate part of Black history. We have a Florida Governor who banned the Advanced Placement course on African/American history because "The content of this course is inexplicably contrary to Florida law, and significantly lacks educational value. (Edweek,2023). Thirty-six states have now introduced bills or taken other actions to restrict how teachers can teach racism and sexism, and 14 states have passed these measures, according to an Education Week analysis. (Edweek, 2022). Teachers are hesitant and reluctant to teach what some see as controversial, and others see as vital history.

In view of Mary's life experiences, it seems so much has not changed. Some laws have changed, but attitudes and practices are still discriminatory and hateful. **I grew up in the South. I grew up with hatred. It's evident in New Orleans. We didn't have the Klan, but we had the White Citizens' Council. We had all Black neighborhoods and schools,**

places you couldn't go, you couldn't eat, sitting behind the sign on the bus.

From day one Mary's family lived in a segregated South—neighborhoods, schools, churches, transportation, movie theaters, public parks —every aspect of life had an awareness of race.

Mary went to all Black schools. She went to a public park to swim that was in a Black neighborhood—no whites swam there. She went to a theater where Blacks sat in the balcony, whites on the main floor. She went to an all-Black university.

Sometimes things were subtle, for example Miss Xavier. Every year a young woman was elected as Miss Xavier. Except for Mary's year, all candidates were light-skinned; dark was not seen to be as pretty. The inference is that lighter is better, especially in Creole New Orleans.

Actress Viola Davis in her best-selling memoir, Finding Me: A Memoir, talked about her struggle to become an actress, particularly as a dark-skinned Black woman. She was a trained actor, acknowledged for her talent, but major roles were not hers because she was "too dark." The role that was her breakthrough was that of a drug-addicted mother who had given up her son in the movie Antwone Fisher. It was a stereotyped role of a welfare mother, the type of role to which she had been confined until people recognized her talent in that film. She went on to become a Triple Award winner with performances in Ma Rainey's Black Bottom, Help, Doubt. Plus, she became the lead in a TV series, How to Get Away with Murder, making her the first Black woman in television history to win an Emmy for best actress in a drama series.

Her journey is only one reminder that racism is still active, opportunities because of skin color are still limited, and the struggle is far from over.

Mary is Creole, meaning she is of Spanish or French European mixed with Black, particularly from the Caribbean region. Her great-grandparents came from the Islands in the Caribbean. She is part French.

Even within Black culture there is a class system. **Growing up, if you are Black and real fair** [complected], **there is a certain group of people who are prejudiced against you, and there is a certain other group who feel you have more advantages because in the South, it was always the thing that the lighter you are, the more accepted or the more comfortable white people would be being around you. There is also a class system in terms of economics, because there was a vein of professional people, doctors, lawyers, schoolteachers; they lived very well and there were a lot of poorer Black kids, too, but we all went to public schools mostly.** (Message Bearer, p. 4)

Laws have often dictated how a person's race is defined. In some states the definition has varied throughout time, and because of slavery, the race of the mother dictated the race of the child. There are places with the "one drop" rule; if a person has one drop of "Black" blood, then they are Black. No other country besides the United States has that rule.

In the South it was 1/16th Black and then your birth certificate said Black. You could look as white as you wanted to, but if you're 1/16th Black...you'd have to go back four generations for that. I say, 'I bet I can line up 12 people and you couldn't pick out the Black people from the white people." And you couldn't. They aren't *all* Black, of course. 1/16th but in terms of birth certificates it says colored. (W-H, p 31)

Hitler's Nazi Germany looked to the United States as an example to follow for our laws on segregation, and miscegenation. The Germans did not just segregate; they decided in The Final Solution which meant extermination. The Germans decided the "one drop" rule was too strict. Instead, the Nazis decreed that a Jewish person was anyone who had a Jewish grandparent. (Nazis, 2023)

Mary's own brother is light-skinned. Mary says he is white. He "passed" for white in the military by his appearance and it gave him certain advantages. No one questioned him because they judged him by his appearance.

Language descriptors also change over time, but the intent is still there. Mary's birth certificate says "colored." Her father's says "Negro."

People can self-categorize on most surveys now. But certain visual aspects still matter in that designation.

Mary was influenced, as are so many, by the movies she saw when she saw people trying to "pass" or biracial couples. Her segregated classrooms were filled with people with all shades of skin color, some people with blond hair, some with light eyes. Yet they were in an all-Black school.

If you go down South, and you look at all these people who were Black who were really from white ancestry, it brings out the South. We used to always say, you know—yes, we had a Mayor Mason. There's a Black Mayor Mason family and a White Mayor Mason family. There was a lot of, not even called mistresses, but just lovers who had children.

Race and mixed heritage are a strong part of the culture in Louisiana and in Mary's hometown of New Orleans. **If you are really connected to the culture and to the community down there, there is no other place that's quite like it, so people just have to get back there, you know, but I wasn't one of those. They talked about his phenomena after Karina—it was almost like "a Katrina Effect." Culture, race, religion, it's everything. You can't separate it. I think that's what it is with people who are really born and raised and love the city of New Orleans—it's not just a racial thing, it's a cultural thing, it's a community thing. There's something about that culture down there that makes them**

whole so that they can't find any other place. I guess I wasn't one of them. (W-H, p 68).

When asked about the fact that Mary does not have a so-called Southern accent, nor does she use stereotypical southern phrase, she said, "**I was always different. I always wondered if I was just dropped into my family. I don't speak like them. My brothers still have a drawl. Most people thought I was Hispanic.** (6th interview, April 15, 2023). Her siblings still live in Louisiana.

People have said that Minnesotans have difficulty talking about race. There is a hidden feeling that "if those people [meaning people of color] would be just like us, everything would be fine." Some people say unusual things because of this discomfort, like the man at the student conference who looked at Mary and said, "You have nice teeth." Huh???? In conversations with Mary, she said everyone in the South knows about race, but the North is also racist just not as overt. "Minnesota Nice" is really an oxymoron; Minnesota nice translates to being more passive-aggressive and using microaggressions.

The history of Minnesota is rife with examples of red lining, a real estate practice, which prevents people of color and Jews from buying homes in certain areas. Only recently have some homeowners been working to strike that language from the covenants of their areas.

In the South, race is not subtle. You just know or someone will let you know. There are no real estate covenants to prohibit buying houses in certain areas, but people know; there are still Jim Crow rules. If someone violates, they suffer consequences. (6th interview, April 15, 2023) In more recent times some wealthier Blacks have been able to buy houses on the Lake now but there is still active segregated housing.

When I first went to Central, the first thing I wanted to do was to increase the number of staff of color in the building. We had a Black math teacher of the time and most of the math department was female at the time, so I thought we had the gender thing done. But then the teacher left. We tried to get Black English teachers in the academic areas but few Black teachers in the upper-level courses. Then we had a Black choir director and teachers of color in science.

There was an urban myth that said Central High School was separated by race—5th floor was for the white kids and progressed down from there. **Part of the community perception was that old rumor that Central was three schools—pregnant girls on first floor, Black kids on second floor, and white kids with gifted programs on top level. That persisted a long time.**

People remarked how the lunchroom seemed divided by race. There was a famous book *Why are all the Black Kids Sitting Together in the Cafeteria* written by Beverly Tatum. She described the human phenomenon to self-select in unknown mixed- race situations by race first, gender second. It was also evident even the school dances at Central which were very well attended by all groups. During the time this author was an assistant principal at Central and supervising dances, the Hmong kids, the Black kids, the white kids seem to dance in their groups, even with some different styles of dancing. At one time the Hmong kids would be in a double circle, girls on the inside, boys behind them and the break dancers would be performing in the middle. The outer circles were to keep Mary from seeing the break dancers, which they were not supposed to do. It did not really work. The white kids would do the Y M CA and the Black kids had their own style. But everybody was there, and they had a lot of fun.

As a principal she had conversations with some of the Black parents about assumed prejudice by white teachers. **She** [a parent] **thought every white teacher there was racist. So, it was a perception that the white teachers did not relate to Black kids or were prejudiced against Black kids. Some of the white teachers were actually better with our Black kids. Some of the white English teachers were great with Black kids. Very fair, very unbiased.**

Mary has experienced racial jealousy. Mary and her colleagues were among the very first recruits from Black colleges to come north. St. Paul did recruit one more year and were successful in hiring three more candidates from Xavier who stayed in the district.

When she and her two colleagues came to Minnesota to teach, they were assigned to the "White" schools when it had been the practice to assign Black teachers to schools with large populations of Black kids. Some teachers felt that their jobs were being taken by these southern transplants who were newcomers to the system.

Skin color was a frequent descriptor—the lighter the better. In New Orleans lighter-skinned Blacks had a certain advantage. In her Creole neighborhood, everybody was considered light skinned, probably because of the French/Spanish/Black combination heritage. Few people were darker than Mary.

She was told not to marry a dark-skinned man. '**Don't marry darker than you because you don't want dark children,' they'd say. But I used to bring the darkest boys in the neighborhood home. My mom would get called over the fence. 'Why is Mary doing this? Can't she find any Creole boys?' But my mom never told me who to date or what to date. There are a lot of color issues among Black people down there, except if the person was rich, then you could cross the Black color line. If you had money and were dark, you could marry somebody who looked lighter because the money status was more the point that the color status at that point. There's a lot of craziness like that among the Black families.** (W-H, p 31)

While she was growing up, if someone tried to "pass" and failed, there could be harsh penalties, such as imprisonment or even death. But some were successful. Mary knew that her neighbor, Miss Goserand **passed to the point where she would not have to give up her seat on the public bus. Most of the women worked in white homes off St. Charles Avenue as maids or domestics. They would take the bus home and we would come from Uptown from school on the bus. We'd get on the bus and there's Miss Goserand sitting in front of the bus. At that time, we were into the Civil Rights Movement, and we would say, "Let's just tell everybody she's Black."** Then I'd say, 'Nah, the woman is tired; just let her sit. If they don't know, that's their problem, not ours.' **We were all mixed color so we would go to the back of the bus, but she'd be sitting right up there.** (W-H, p. 32)

Segregation was a daily factor of life. On every public transit there was a sign "For Coloreds Only.' She and others would be responsible for moving the sign forward and back, to section off the seating, when whites boarded the bus. These are the signs already described in an earlier chapter. **But you know what? It was part of the way of life, so you didn't even question it. They'd say, 'You need to move.' And if there were seats behind you, you moved, otherwise you were arrested."** (W-H, p. 32)

Being arrested or even being stopped by the police was something Mary feared. When asked about the police, Mary's response. **I feared them.** (6th interview April 15, 2023) This discussion led into talking about George Floyd. When asked about her reaction to his murder, **Coming from the South, nothing surprises me. Violence from the police didn't surprise me. What surprised me was that there were white protesters in the crowds. In the South that wouldn't have happened. It would have just been Black protesters."** (6th interview, April 15, 2023).

Even though she personally fears police, she currently has two nephews who are on the New Orleans police force.

As mentioned earlier even at her all-Black Xavier University, skin color mattered. Miss Xavier who was chosen by popular votes, was always light-skinned, except, Mary says proudly, during her year. The candidate was darker than usual which was an accomplishment.

In a personal conversation with another educated Black woman whose father had graduated from Xavier as well, the woman told Mary that she (Mary) would have been someone her dad might have dated. Mary replied, "Because I'm light-skinned." The woman agreed.

During her experiences in Selma, racism was a constant factor. The house mother where the group stayed was white and pregnant. Because she volunteered at the church that supported Blacks, the woman had to give birth in the hospital relegated to Blacks. **You think about things like that and think, those things really happened? As a white person if you associated with someone Black—you might as well have been Black. If you were white and involved in the Civil Rights Movement, helping Black people, you were now Black as far as the white people were concerned. They treated you like you were Black.** (W-H, p. 54).

The priest in charge of this experience, Father Woulette, was white. He was under the threat of excommunication from the Catholic Church at the hands of a racist bishop because Father Woulette helped church clergy participate in the March from Selma to Montgomery.

He had opened the gymnasium to all the clergy who came down South. He offered them sleeping arrangements in the gym and Bishop Toolin found out and didn't like it. He was bishop of all Catholic schools and churches in the state of Alabama. Fr. Woulette was a member of the Edwinite order, not diocesan, but a separate order

working in the state and so [the] dictate from the Bishop was that either Fr. Woulette left the state because of his cooperation with that March or the Bishop was going to kick out the entire order. So, Fr. Woulette packed up and left. (W-H, p, 55)

Ever the activist, Mary and her college classmates even wrote Pope Paul pleading Fr. Woulette's case. They never got a reply. Therefore, they decided to organize a Kneel-in at the white Catholic church in Selma. **I don't know why we did this in Selma. The four of us went to the church. Now tell me we weren't crazy. We were scared.** (W-H, p. 55)

Mary and her friends would experience hatred just walking in the street or going to school because of their racially mixed group. **People would spit at us especially when I was walking with a student from Boston University. I did go to the Litle Brown Church hoping to hear Martin Luther King, but he didn't show up. Rev. Abernathy spoke. It was really the heyday of the Civil Rights Movement. It was exciting to be a part of it. Scary, though. Selma was scary—especially for Black people. The Klan was prominent; they'd march through the street, and they had lynching offices. It was completely segregated with lots of Jim Crow laws. They had separate schools at that point. I had never really lived in fear like that in terms of being Black in the South. In New Orleans you live in our own Black community, you're insulated. You never have to leave if you don't want to – church, schools, everything** is right there. You've got to go shopping downtown but you always realize you have to sit in the back of the bus, or you weren't going to be waited on until everybody else is waited on in a store or restaurant. So, you adjusted yourself to those things, but not like this—not scary. (W-H, p. 55)

Mary was determined to face the bishop herself to speak for Fr. Woulette. She decided to visit him herself. **I knocked on the door, but nobody answered but I was going to talk to him, at least try to reason with him. His house was there, and it was close to the bus stop. He lived in one of those big old Victorian mansions. Nobody answered the door. That was quite an experience.**

Even though I was born and raised in the South, I wasn't born and raised in what they call the Deep South in terms of how much worse off other people were in terms of being Black and coming from a little small town like that [Selma]. It made me realize what we were fighting for after that. I was scared but defiant because of the action. We were a mixed group so we were opening ourselves up to something terrible by maybe we also knew that Selma was in the limelight of the news and hoped that maybe nothing [bad] would happen. (W-H, p. 57)

Because of this taste of political action, when she returned to Xavier, she became involved in helping work for Lyndon Johnson's presidential campaign. She was also editor of the school newspaper and got involved in the National Student Association which was very politically involved. She participated in several student conferences as well. Her first trip north was to a student conference at the University of Madison Wisconsin, a hotbed at that time of political activism. It was a summer conference. **I thought I'd died and gone to heaven—there was a big lake in the middle of this college. And a bar—the Rathskeller. There was a bar right on campus.** (W-H, p. 57)

Then she attended an annual conference in Washington, D.C. in 1965 as things were heating up in the Civil Rights Movement. She travelled alone for the first time to Washington D.C. What an experience.

After university she moved to Minnesota. When she was first living in St. Paul, once she was recruited to attend parties with football players to be the dates for the Black players. Some coaches did not want players dating white women. But the players dated white women anyway.

In fact, which is how she met her to-be- husband, Earsell Mackbee, who was a Viking football player whom she met at a party. They were not serious right away but reconnected and were married less than a year after they started dating. Some people criticized her for marrying someone darker than she was. But that did not matter to Mary.

When they bought a house in Bloomington, they were the only Black family in the neighborhood. Their children attended Bloomington Public Schools, eventually graduating from Bloomington Kennedy which was mostly a school of white students at the time. **When we moved into our house, people made cute jibes. For example, we had a Norwegian Elkhound, one of those curly-tailed dogs, and the neighbor boy wanted to know if our dog was Black too. I said, 'No, he's Norwegian."** (3rd interview, February 16, 2023)

Relationships and Marriage

Women in educational administration often talk about toll that this difficult and time-consuming position takes on personal and family relationships, especially if there are young children involved. Many women who become administrators, particularly at the secondary or district levels, do so at an older age compared to men, often waiting until their children are older and a little more self-sufficient. Men can work when their children at any age. Single and divorced women are common. A sort of sarcastic complaint in women's groups is that "I need a wife." As sexist as that comment is, what it means is that even if someone has the best partner in the world, the responsibility for childcare and maintaining daily needs in the house, like laundry, remain in the domain of women. Mary is quoted earlier about the women in the District Office in St. Paul as being mostly unmarried.

The job takes a toll on relationships, especially if you've got a partner that's insecure. I think that was it. A lot of the divorced women I know, I think, were married to this type of man. I think that was me then. When I finally asked for a divorce, my soon-to-be ex-husband

wrote me a two-page typewritten note which I should have kept but didn't. In it he called me an 'administrative bitch.' I don't know what that means but that's what he called me. It does take a toll.

Part of the strain is that administrators talk about losing their privacy. One is always on exhibit, being looked at and watched as a role model. For Mary, **the good news for me was I worked in St. Paul but lived in Bloomington, so people weren't privy to my private life. I would shop and be at school and was probably in St. Paul more than Bloomington, but my private life was a distance away. It also helped, I think, that my children didn't go to the school. People didn't know about my kids, my family, my house. My private life was separate, and I liked it that way. I didn't move closer because I needed a separate identity--one as a building principal, and then one as a mother in Bloomington.** (2nd interview, February 8, 2023) It is more difficult to maintain a private life if one becomes a superintendent because many communities expect the superintendent to live in the community where the person is visible while shopping, in church, and even exercising. But privacy is necessary for people to relax and recharge. It is sometimes hard to chisel that out of an educational leader's day.

Marriage

Early in her career there was an undercurrent that **It [a woman in an educational leadership job] was mostly like taking a man's job and then,** of course, now, having a man's hours—you're away from home more. Especially at the high school level—a lot of evening activities and just the time away from home where you can't take care of your family because you're in this leadership position and your hours are longer. You're not just a teacher; you're not going home and cooking dinner every day. There just seemed to be a lot of the women who were either single and never married, or married and got divorced while they were working on their administrative degree or working. (W-H, p. 81)

Even during the years of her marriage, for most of that time she was the only breadwinner. Earsell could no longer play football because of an injury and had off and on had part-time jobs. Mary's salary was what they counted on. Later as a single parent Mary was the one who paid all the bills. She received no child support and no physical presence to help with supervision, as eventually Earsell did not live in the same city. She knew she was not home a lot, but she told her children that they all had a choice—food, and clothes or Mary being home.

Her marriage to Earsell was often a source of worry. Earsell was born in 1941 in Mississippi. When they met, he was in his second season with the Minnesota Vikings. In retrospect, she is surprised that she married him. He was divorced, she was young. Plus, Earsell was telling people, bragging really, that he was going to marry a schoolteacher. For him, Mary was a real catch.

They moved into a home in Bloomington. Mary had a full-time job teaching position but no money in the bank. He was still a Viking which only lasted two years, **Earsell was making more than me. I was making $7000, and he was probably making $30,000 so it looked like a whole lot, but the football players weren't making big money like now. Many people don't know it, but they weren't paid during the off season, not like now where they make hundreds of thousands, or millions of dollars. The only person that made big money was the quarterback, Fran Tarkington—he was probably making a million.** (W-H, p. 70). **They earned nothing in the summertime. When they played those pre-season games, they got 70 bucks a week, $10 a day because they were giving them room and board.** (2nd interview, February 8, 2023)

Being a "Viking wife" put Mary in a whole different lifestyle. At the time she was the only wife of the players who had a full-time job. **When you're in It, [the athletic lifestyle], it's kind of glamorous, but then there are all the pitfalls. At the time, some were heavy drinkers, some were drug users, and then you had the Christian athletes on one side who were pure and all about family and religion. That wasn't my guy—no. That wasn't my group. These were rough and tough players. They were hard drinkers, hard livers, there were affairs, and groupies.** (W-H, p. 71)

Earsell was never what one would call faithful. There were relationships before, during, and after his marriage to Mary. Her conservative, Catholic upbringing did not prepare her for the groupies that were always there, for example. **When the players were out of town, you didn't know what the heck was going on. There were always groupies. You didn't even have to go out of town, just go to Mankato** [where the training grounds were]—**you'd see a hotel receipt in the car or something.** (W-H, p. 71.

There were often late-night parties, especially on Sunday nights after games. Because Mary had to get up on Monday morning and teach, she would attend the parties but sometimes she found places even behind a couch where she could go to sleep. Plus, the whole drinking atmosphere was not her style.

It became increasingly obvious that things were not going well in the marriage. She tried hard to make the marriage work. **There were hard times. I remember we were talking, and this is before we had children, and I knew it wasn't going well. I said, 'This is not working—you're fooling around and this and that.' And he said, 'Well, there's no excitement in this marriage' or something like that. I thought about what I can do to make it exciting. For some reason I thought of playing horseshoes. So, I went out and bought a set of horseshoes. I naively thought the game would spice up the relationship. When I think of that now, I have to laugh. Horseshoes????** (W-H, p. 72 and 3rd interview, February 16, 2023). When asked if the marriage fell apart because of her work, Mary replied, **No, I think it was because of his philandering more than anything.** (2nd interview, February 8, 2023).

In 1969 the Vikings played in the Super Bowl in New Orleans and lost. Wives were not allowed to travel with the team, so family members had to travel and find their own lodging. The structure of the team was not supportive to developing family life and structure. In fact, the opposing team, the Kansas City Chiefs, was more forward thinking. (W-H, p. 73)

The Kansas City Chiefs stayed in the French Quarter at the Royal Senesta; the wives were with them, but Bud Grant [coach] said, 'No.' He was of the old theory that sex before a game would drain their energy. The Vikings stayed out by the airport. Honest to God, they almost missed getting to the stadium on time because the traffic was so horrid. They were coming from 30 miles away. (W-H, p. 73)

Mary was working at St. Louis Park at that time. At the end of the school year, they decided to start having a family. Because Mary had not gotten pregnant so far, they decided to adopt. For some reason Earsell thought it would be fun to adopt twins. I found out later he had twins in California. Twins were not available, but they got Myles who was two months old and Mylo who was just eleven days old. Myles had a hernia when he was born. At this point Earsell was injured and was picked up by the Pittsburgh Steelers. His knee injury never healed, and he was released the same year. Mary was home for four months with the babies, the only time she was ever not working outside the home. She found herself with two young children, an unemployed husband, and nothing to fall back on.

Those were struggling days. I called my former AP who was Assistant Superintendent at the time and asked if I could come back to St. Paul in January. In January 1971 I was assigned to Como Park Junior High. (W-H, p. 74)

The infant boys went to day care. Two and a half years later, Mary gave birth to Mateo Rey, their third son. Five years later in 1978, Marcee Dee was born. Earsell never worked much. He did small jobs, sold cars but made little money. If he ever got a paycheck, he kept the whole thing, not contributing to household expenses. **I remember one time when he got paid, I said to him,' Are you going to give me some of your money to pay the bills? Because I'm even paying your car bill, you know.' He said he would see what he could do. I got nothing.**

Of course, one of the worst things that could happen, happened to me. I was at the District Office at the time and one of the guys in Finance that I knew well called me. He said, 'Mary, you've got to come down. There is an issue. Your wages are being garnished.' I said, 'What for?' He said, 'For the loan you have at Marquette National Bank in Minneapolis.' I said, 'I don't have anything going with Marquette National Bank.' Earsell had taken out a loan and had a girlfriend forge my name on the document and got a car. He wasn't paying the car note so they garnished my wages. I said, 'I never signed anything.' I had to get an attorney to prove it wasn't my signature, which an attorney was something I really couldn't afford. (2nd interview, February 8, 2023)

Mary managed the house and just afforded basic maintenance, daycare, food, etc. The house deteriorated for a while because there was no money.

Years later I finally read an article about monogamous husbands and husbands that are just not equipped to have one mate and then finally I just said, 'You know, it's not me at all—it's you. You just can't accept this kind of a relationship.' So, once I had that realization, which was years later—we were married for 19 years, but it took me 18 years to come to that conclusion. (W-H, p. 75)

In 1989 the couple separated, and Earsell left Minnesota, leaving Mary on her own with four children, the youngest of whom was eleven-year-old Marcee. In many ways Mary had been a single parent for many years. After five years of separation, Mary filed for divorce. **The only reason I went ahead with the divorce was because the house was paid off. For the first time and I thought 'I've got to get this thing in my own name so I could get another loan to fix it up.'** (W-H, p. 75)

I had to work because in the 19 years he only worked half of that time. It was difficult. It was a struggle. One day I looked up and I said, 'Well, I never wanted to be a statistic. I didn't want to be a single black mother raising, you know, black children. But I thought that's exactly what I'm doing. And I'm raising a fifth child who's 40 years old, you know. I got a divorce. (2nd interview, February 8, 2023)

He tried to fight me for the house, even though I had made all the payments. Eventually he was served with papers. The judge told him he had to pack his things and leave and not to take anything with him. In spite of that, I came home from school one day, and there was a trailer pulled up to the house. He took everything out of the living room. I said, "Just go. Just take it. Whatever. Just you go with it.' It wasn't worth the fight. At the time he was supposed to give me $250 every two weeks. I can remember Marcee and I sitting right on the stoop when we got the first $250. I looked at her and I said, 'We're going to splurge because I know this is going to be it. I know this will be it.' It was. He quit his job, which at the time was managing or working in a high rise in Minneapolis which is also where he lived.

He never paid any more child support. $250. That was it. When by the time Mylo died and Marcy was 18, he was $52,000 in arrears. I didn't sue. There was nothing to sue. He left town a little later and went to California. When we had our first divorce hearing downtown, I remember I got dressed up. I got dressed up to get married so I'm getting dressed up to get divorced.

He didn't show up. The judge said, 'Well, I could file in your favor, but he can appeal one time.' I said, 'No, let's reschedule.' because I had a feeling he wasn't going to show up because he was out of town. In fact, his attorney said he hadn't even contacted the attorney yet. So, the second time we met, he didn't show. I got the house by default.

At the divorce we took his name off the title. Before the divorce was final once he was back in town for a graduation or something. One of the kids asked if he could stay in the basement. I said, 'Sure.' When he was here, we talked about him not paying child support. He said, "How can I?' I said, "You can sign over the house.' He said, 'Over my dead body.' I said, 'That can be arranged.' I had paid the mortgage all those years but because he didn't show up for that second hearing, he lost by default, and I got the house. (2nd interview, February 8, 2023) **I got everything, which I deserved because I was the one paying for it all, all those years anyway.** (W-H, p. 76)

Throughout the marriage money was an issue. Mary was the breadwinner. Earsell would repeatedly ask her for money. He would steal money from her wallet to spend on who knows what. At one point Mary slept on her purse so he could not steal from her when she was asleep. He would write checks on her account. **Once I remember sleeping behind the couch with my purse. He would take my checkbook and write checks. I don't** know how I survived. Honestly, now that I think back because our house was foreclosed on once because I couldn't pay the mortgage which was about $300/month at that time. I was a teacher making about $8000 a year. I remember the sheriff coming to the door with a foreclosure notice because of back mortgage payments. I ran to the local teacher credit union, Federal Credit Union, to borrow money to pay the mortgage. I don't know how we kept up with it after that, but I did. I always worked at summer school too because we were only paid ten months a year and I had to have money coming in.

I've actually paid for this house three times. The first time with the first mortgage which I think was around $25,000, I've refinanced and used the assets for college, weddings, etc. (2nd interview, February 8, 2023).

What did I do with the children? Well, he wasn't working so he was in charge. He had to take Marcee to school because he still wasn't working. That was only while the kids were fairly young. (2nd interview, February 8, 2023)

One of the ways Mary has economized is that she has always driven old cars. **Never could afford a new one.** (2nd interview, February 8, 2023) At Central High School there was a class on auto mechanics held in a garage owned by the school and taught by a wonderfully skilled man named Ed Roth. Sometimes people would get the students to overhaul cars. Or cars might be donated as a tax deduction; students could fix them and sell them for money to support the program. If a decent car became available, Ed would sometimes let Mary know, especially if her car was causing problems. There were several times that Mary would call school and say she was broken down; someone would get her and tow the car. She tells a story where once a visitor parked in the staff lot at the back of the school. There was a beat-up car in the principal's spot. When the guest asked where the principal was going to park, the guest was told that the principal was already parked right there. Tactfully, the guest said nothing.

Divorce is a sadness, no matter how you look at it, no matter how problematic the relationship is. For Mary it was no different. **I'm not sure it was ever love. I don't think I knew what love was. When I met him, I was naïve. I was naïve when I married him, and he was worldly and just a total womanizer. I was lonely, had just broken up with my boyfriend. He was making money at the time. My family was excited. He was a football player at the time, a popular kind of guy. The neighbors raised their eyebrows, and my mother was told I was darkening the neighborhood. because he was darker than me, but my family didn't care** (W-H, p.76)

Later in life when Earsell had some health issues, including several strokes, Mary severed ties with him for fear of having to become his caretaker. **I severed it. But my children—if they need help, I've helped**

them get power of attorney. I can't go back because knowing me, I'd want to take charge. I'll support them, but I can't be involved in his life—that *was* **a past chapter.** (W-H, p. 76)

When Earsell died, he wanted to be buried in California. But he had no money. The Vikings and NFL actually paid to have the body shipped to California on what was called a "mercy flight." Mary did not pay for the funeral but paid for the three kids, by this time son Mylo had passed, to attend. To quote Mary '**These fathers…You can't pick them.**' (2nd interview, February 8, 2023).

When asked about having relationships after her divorce, she said people had tried to set her up with dates. One she remembers that it was a double date with a nice man but there was "no chemistry." She did not really have the time to have a relationship. Plus, she said, **the last thing I need is a man."**

First Year as Central's Principal

Transitions are difficult. As a school administrator moving to a new site is always a balance of learning the new culture, examining what is working well and supporting it, naming what needs to change and doing it, and building a sense of community. Many years ago, Jennifer James, a cultural anthropologist, spoke to a group of school administrators and remarked that when one is in the first six months in any new organization, that is the time one has the clearest vision of the assets and flaws of the organization. After six months one has become part of that organization and has begun to "drink the Kool-Aid," and the vision is not as sharp.

Another factor in a transition is to consider what type of leader one is following. From this author's experience it makes a difference if one is replacing a well-liked person or one whom everyone was glad to see leave. If one is following a well-liked person, people will be comparing every move to the sometimes glorified and amplified successes or popular ideas of the predecessor. This is particularly difficult if some of those things that are popular are things that need to change. The stories of the well-liked leader seem to take on a rosy glow as people forget the person's faults. People feel that change is disrespectful to the person they really liked so they can be resistant.

If one is following someone who is not liked, then one has a temporary halo because people believe that nirvana has arrived. However, when nirvana fails to materialize, grumblings start, and the leader is faced with building constructive relationships based on new behaviors.

Each type has its blessings and curses. Mary followed a person who was not very present. Mary's hand-on, very physical presence was a significant change. But her first year was tough.

Mary's first year at Central was a hurdle that tested her mettle and sent the message to staff, students, and community as to the type of leader she was. She came as she said, **under a cloud. When I came in 93,** everyone knew I had been demoted from the District Office. I guess I had something to prove. I could still be a good leader. That first year was traumatic. (5th interview, March 21, 2023).

One of the major incidents that first year was a riot. I was at the University of Minnesota for a function, came back and Marshall [the street Central lives on] was cordoned off from the tennis courts to Lexington Avenue. They had to let the bus come in to get the kids out. There was a big riot in the cafeteria. Kids were pushing Officer Brown, the police liaison, around. About 50 kids, I don't know what the issue was, but they went on a rampage during lunchtime and just held the school. The secretary had dialed 911. The police aggravated the situation because police cars came, including dogs, and the scene became more polarized. I worked with her [the secretary] and told her never to dial 911. We could handle it by dealing with the students. If we needed more help from the police, we had a different number to call that did not precipitate the calls going out over all police radios and the ensuing media coverage.

Unfortunately, the police got the brunt of that for over-reaction. The NAACP, and everybody was on their case for over-reacting to an urban school just because there are Black kids there. We came off okay because the police were criticized for over-responding. In their defense they made the 911 call public. When it was played, it made their case for a full-scale response. It was a frantic call—a frantic call, highly emotional.

Mary and district officials held two community meetings to help mediate the perception that Police Chief Finney and his officers had overreacted due to the race of the students. **They didn't help themselves because as they were talking, they said, 'Well, when we respond we're taught to shoot for body mass.' We were amazed at that and said, 'Oh, God, you didn't need to go there; we're not going to kill anyone.** (W-H, p 99)

Another incident later was that there was supposedly an intruder with a gun at Central. Of course, we followed a procedure but again, it put Central in the news and caused a lot of fright, commotion, and disruption. However, as said in the newspapers the next day, "No gun at Central."

Every principal knows that the relationship with the head secretary is particularly important because that person is the right hand of the principal. Staff members often say that the secretary runs the school and there is some truth to that. Before Mary came to Central, **she** [the secretary] **heard that I treated my secretaries badly. I said, 'You didn't hear that because my secretaries were my confidantes. I trusted them. They were my associates. I didn't treat them badly. I treated one badly because she** was a crook. But, no, you heard wrong.' She kind of eased up. I worked hard with her because our styles were different.

I also had a minus coming from the District. I remember my opening speech to the staff. I acknowledged the feelings about coming from the District and that I hadn't been in the schools for seven years. But as I told them then, being a principal is the best job I've ever had. I plan on doing a good job with your help. That's how we started. We're in this together. We have a job to build the reputation of the school back to where it was, (5th interview, March 21, 2023)

Death of a Child

Mylo was born on July 30, 1970. Mylo had lots of curly dark hair and was always the more artsy one between him and Myles who was adopted the same day. It is possible that Mylo had fetal alcohol effect because he had some difficulty with attachment. **I remember once we had a fight, he looked at me and said, 'You're not my mother.' I replied, 'I'm the only mother you've got.' Mylo was a little detached.**

In 1992 Mylo had a motorcycle accident which resulted in his being a quadriplegic, paralyzed from the chest down, confined to a wheelchair. He was hospitalized for a while. At the time Mary was working full-time and Marcee was the only child living at home.

Mary decided that he would get good care in a nursing home in Minneapolis. However, **I was there one day when the guy (PCA) was telling him to sit up. Mylo tried to but, of course, he couldn't. The attendant put him in his chair and that was all. Mylo was fully cognizant in his mind but just not physically. That place was not conducive to somebody who still had a mind. We brought him home. Friends built a ramp; we enlarged the door so the wheelchair could pass through into my bedroom in the back so he could have the Personal Care Attendant have access to water.**

I then moved into the second bedroom. Marcee was in high school most of the time but was around to help too, especially on weekends. She was actually considered his PCA (personal care attendant), **so she was paid rather than hiring a stranger. It allowed her to earn some money for college.**

Marcee and I basically took care of him on weekends. But it was hard. We had to get him into his chair, turn him, do toileting, bathe him. It was hard, physical work.

During this time Mary realized she had to maintain strength, particularly upper body strength, to be able to lift and move him. She joined a fitness club and began lifting weights several times a week. She would leave school after a full day which would start early, work a full day, go lift weights, then go home to take care of Mylo. It was a stressful time. Upon reflection, she wondered how she did it. But one does what one must do.

It was a hard time having him at home. He had a bitter attitude and many episodes of anxiety. He'd whip out of here at midnight in his electric wheelchair, go in the circle [in the road] **and spin in his wheelchair. He would be just obstinate and very belligerent. The neighbors were so good. One night when I came home, he wasn't there. I said, 'Where in the hell is he?" He had gone to the video store which he liked to do. I waited. And I waited. And I waited. And he never came home.**

I went to the video store, and he was still there. I said, 'It's time to go. It's dark. You know you don't have a light on your wheelchair. Follow me home' And he did for a while. Then we got to 98th Street. I told him I'd meet him at home because he was now on the sidewalk.

But he never got home. About half an hour later, I thought, where in the hell is he? He had fallen over in his wheelchair down by the creek. We think he fell because that part of the sidewalk was uneven. We called 911 and they finally found him. He died soon after because we think he had a stroke. (2nd interview, February 8, 2023)

Mylo died in 1997 at the age of 26.

In later times when things were hard, Mary would say, "**What can happen? The worst that could happen has already happened to me** [the death of a child] **and I survived.**

DEmotion that became a PROmotion

Few people can turn a traditionally negative event into one that became one of the most positive events that lasted 25 years. But Mary Mackbee did.

Curman Gaines, once Superintendent of St. Paul Public Schools, is a key player in this drama because he and Mary started as relative peers and later Curman became her boss as the superintendent. In 1984 Mary was chosen to be the principal of the Jefferson Alternative-Career Study Center which was her first head principalship. Curman Gaines was also a candidate partly because he was male and he had experience as the assistant principal at the Center. However, Mary was chosen. Instead, Curman was sent to Hazel Park as principal when he thought he had the job at Jefferson.

Next, in 1987 Superintendent David Bennett asked Mary to take the interim position as Director of Secondary Teaching and Learning. The following June the job was posted, she applied and got it which created hard feelings with another female Black administrator in the district, who felt she should have had the position because of her previous district level experience. Shortly thereafter she left St. Paul but there were hard feelings because she wanted that job. She was told that the reason she did not get the job was because she did not have experience as a principal, so the Superintendent put her at Harding for three months as principal, replacing Mary. She too later became Mary's boss.

At this point Curman Gaines became Superintendent of St. Paul Public Schools. As Director of Secondary Teaching and Learning, Mary worked hard with a colleague who had gotten the position of Director of Elementary Teaching and Learning. The two worked well together, for example, and were responsible, for example, for bringing American Indian program to St. Paul. When her colleague was hired, Curman placed him on the salary schedule—two levels above Mary. Mary wrote Dr. Gaines a letter stating her case, that she had been hired for the position first, it was an equal position, and was cause for a discrimination suit. She felt the remedy would be that she would be placed on the same salary level retroactive to when she started. Curman agreed. He did it.

Some members of the Black community had a different lifestyle that Mary could not afford and chose not to belong to. During that time she had a friendly relationship with Curman and his wife who often attended wedding anniversary parties and other events. But **I still don't hang with those groups. I never see myself as one of them. I guess I was still that poor little girl from New Orleans.** (W-H, p. 89). **It wasn't my lifestyle.**

Soon Mary and her colleague got demoted to Assistant Directors. Mary thought it was because they did not **kowtow to Curman. I remember** him telling us our job was to make him look good. I said, 'That's not my job. My job is to make the principals look good. If you are the Superintendent and you're not doing what's right, it's not right and I'm not going to be loyal.' (1st interview, January 31, 2023) Her senses of right and wrong and fairness are guiding principles which she lives by.

When I was Director at a budget meeting one time, I was just livid because they were going to cut 35 million out of our secondary budget. And I said, 'No. If you're going to cut it out of my budget, you have to cut it out of other's too. Most people do not stand up to the Superintendent or Budget Director. I guess I upset Curman. (1st interview, January 31, 2023)

Later Curman decided to demote both Mary and her colleague from Director to Assistant Director by one level claiming he needed to make room for a new Assistant Director of Curriculum. The rationale was that they would no longer have any curricular responsibilities.

They claimed we could be demoted, so we were demoted. We weren't sure of the reason. The Special Education Director, Bernie Dailey, bless his heart –we were at a retreat, and he said, "You know, you should have demoted me too." He was the only other Director, and he said, 'I really feel bad that I wasn't part of this demotion because that's what's good for the group.' I think that was our demise, actually, for both of us. (W-H, p.92)

Later that year Mary and her colleague were demoted even further out of District Office entirely. For Mary it was the final blow to her career at the District Office. **It's really interesting because we never knew why. We never knew if it was me and my colleague who got caught up in some behind the scenes interactions we knew nothing about. I was well liked among the principals I served. Maureen Flanagan, Superintendent Gaines' executive assistant, was down there at that time. I often blamed it on her though now she's one of my best friends. I really never knew what got me into this situation.**

Ironically, the new Curriculum Director, Carol Sorenson, was unaware of the demotion. **Carol knew nothing about it and** [when she found out she] **was opposed to it. But it was Curman's decision. She was not in favor of it because she knew the backlash was going to happen. We were both very popular leaders at that point.** (W-H, p. 92)

Mary wondered if her popularity was indeed her downfall. She was a compassionate supervisor who was always willing to lend a hand to those who served. Yet in the Board of Education's resolution, it stated that the demotions were a result of a need for new leadership which struck Mary as an invalid excuse. (W-H, p. 92)

Maybe I was too connected to our groups and that Curman didn't like that. I don't know. I know that at the end of the year, all the principals signed a letter, except for one colleague—I'll never forget

that—that they had no problems with my leadership and couldn't understand the need for change. The Board Resolution said that the reason I was being demoted was that they wanted new leadership, new energy. It was strange. It said that I was demoted Without Cause, meaning they didn't have a cause. As a result of this, in the superintendency members' contract right now, it states that you can be demoted with a 30-day notice with or without cause. (W-H, p. 93)

What was the meeting with Curman like that told them they were being demoted? **My colleague and I were arguing as we usually do— he would ask, 'What time is the meeting this morning?' I'd say, 'It's 8:00'. 'No, Mary, it's at 8:30.' 'No, it's at 8.' 'No, Mary, it's at 8:30' I went to the secretary and Rosie told me that 'Mary, yours is at 8, his is at 8:30' I went back, and I told him, 'We're going to get fired.' Honestly-- and that's what it was.** (W-H, p. 93)

At that meeting Mary took the news badly because she was unable to understand what she had done wrong. **Curman said, 'I've thought about it and we're going to demote both of you. We need this new leadership; we need this new energy and so your job will end as of June 30th.' Me? I'm an emotional person—I just couldn't say anything. I got up and walked out and slammed the door behind me, not intentionally but it's just that you're trying to get out of there as fast as you can so you can

go bawl some place. I went back to my colleague, and I said 'I got fired. I think you're next.' (W-H, p. 94)

Because of her reaction, the rumor circulated that she had handled it poorly, my colleague supposedly had handled it well. **People around us were very compassionate, they couldn't understand it either. We got nice compliments. We never found out the exact reason why we all of a sudden were in Curman's disfavor.** (W-H, p. 94)

People wondered who would replace Mary. Maureen Flanagan, Curman's white administrative assistant, was mentioned. She and Curman took a lot of flak.

Mary had a month to clean up and prepare to move on to her next assignment. **It was the end of the year; most of the principals were gone. We had a nice send-off, and the administrative group gave me a plaque—my big leadership plaque with the state of Minnesota from my own group. That meant more to me than Curman at that point because I felt that at least the people whom I worked for felt I had done a good job.** (W-H, p. 95)

To mark the changes, they held a big going away party in a colleague's backyard as a thank you to the principals and colleagues of the past years. Mary's friendship with Curman was rocky, to say the least, if not over.

Many of her colleagues were angry about it. Other educators even got into the public discussion, including Charlie Kyte, Executive Director of Minnesota Association of School Administrators. There had been an article published in the newspaper, " 'so and so' and Mackbee demoted to Principal." Charlie Kyte wrote a response to that arguing that the principal position is the most key role in any school district.

Charlie wrote that a principalship was not a demotion; it was the most important job because it was directly related to kids. In fact, I carried that little article, that little thing, in my planner for years.

At our Fall Administrative Retreat it was standard practice to announce job changes. That year when Curman stood and said, "All of you who received a promotion, stand up; I thought about that article and I thought 'This is a privilege, being a principal;' so I stood up and the whole group in attendance just erupted with applause—it caused Superintendent Gaines some embarrassment actually. (W-H, p. 91)

Mary's act of standing up demonstrated her strength of character, courage, and belief in herself and in her ability to be a quality educator. Her peers respected her for it.

I didn't hate him, but I thought....my rule is always, when you do people wrong, God will get you in the end. You'll get your own one of these days. When I finally met with him again, I just said, 'Here's what I want—again. I want my vacation paid, I want this, and I want that." I

negotiated my exit in terms of money, so I got all my vacation. (W-H, p. 95) Once again Mary challenged unfair past practices.

Her colleague could, and did, retire; Mary needed a job. She had always liked being a principal. The only principal opening that year was at Central. **I thought, that's fine. I can go back to being a principal. It's a good job. It's one I love doing so it wasn't out of my bailiwick. My final act as director was to appoint myself to Central High School.** (W-H, p. 96)

Even though Mary said she "**hated Curman for a while.**" Curman obviously had respect for her. About a year and a half after she started at Central, **Curman called me and asked me to meet for breakfast. I thought he really can't fire me anymore, so I went to breakfast. He offered me a job in his Cabinet. It was in professional development. I said, "No, that's not my forte.' I realized I was back where I belonged. I love being a building principal. I said, 'it's the best job I've ever had and I'm going to stay there. No thank you.'** (5th interview, April 15, 2023)

Enter Principal Mackbee......

Many of us have hurdles, or some would call them learning experiences, which create our character. Some believe failure is a natural learning experience. Others may say that which does not kill you, makes you stronger. All those things are probably true, but when living through traumatic, difficult times, it's difficult to see the sunshine through the window or to smell the spring lilacs.

Mary is no different. When looking at her challenges and hurdles, it is apparent that she has had major ones. If rated on a scale of 1 to 10, the number would be at least a 9, with 10 being death. Daily overt and covert racism, sexism, losing a child, being publicly discounted by being promoted from a position where one is respected and seen as doing an excellent job are all very major traumas. Divorce, although more common, is also a major trauma.

Yet Mary will say, **"The worst has already happened to me. I have survived and will continue to do so."**

CHAPTER SIX

Values and Assets

Mary, like most people, is a complex woman who has experienced many difficult events, euphemistically called 'growing pains', and many positive supports that have helped build the resilience she demonstrates. So far our journey has taken us from Mary's early upbringing to looking at the history of Central High School which Mary led for 25 years and then to the challenges she has faced. Throughout those journeys Mary developed and used her values and assets which is the topic of this chapter.

It is difficult to list all the things someone values, and of course, this is being done by observers, not necessarily by Mary herself. Observers may, in fact, treasure and find some things remarkable that the person takes for granted and others see as unique or valuable. Let's begin…..

Believes people are important

We have seen over and over how Mary has said she believes in people, starting with her family. **Maybe it's culture because growing up, having a big family, there was always somebody there. There was always an uncle or somebody staying with us, or my brothers would have their grandchildren or their children, mostly grandchildren. There's always somebody staying with us. I had two of my husband's**

brothers living with me at one time. My sister was here for a summer but she didn't stay long.

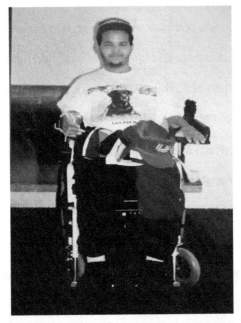

Mylo

Myles and wife Shawn, Blake, Makel, Peyton, Mateo, Myles Jr. Brandon, Erin, Mykael, Lauren, Mary, Xavier, Livy, Marcee

She prioritizes when it comes to where she spends her time, energy, and money. She takes care of her family first, whether it's helping with college, letting them live with her temporarily when they need it, babysitting children, dogs, cats, or even buying diapers. She cared for handicapped son while working full-time and worked out to maintain muscle strength to be able to care for him. That was a priority.

She stood up for family as a young girl when she stood up to the boys who wanted to take Joe's bike. She and Joe did not let them, even though he did not want help from his little sister.

As she is now the matriarch, she hosts all holidays at her house for those who can come and eat traditional dishes. Recently, before Easter as Mary and her granddaughter are cooking up a storm, someone wrote in chalk on the sidewalk in front of her door "For Good Food Enter Here". That's how the family sees her.

Her family knows they can count on her whether it's to help bring a supply of fresh oysters to Mateo's restaurant or to babysit pets when needed. **I've never had an empty nest. Somebody is always living here. I've never minded it.** (4th interview, March 7, 2023_

Beyond her biological family Mary believed in creating a community, also with food, in her places of work. As she told the Central staff in her opening speech, "We're in this together." Mary valued all members of the staff. Mary often could be found with the custodians during their break having coffee. She brought treats often. She knew them, their families. Plus, she loved talking to the "lunch ladies." They were a fun group and Mary would often hang out in the kitchen, again knowing each of the women (they were always women) and their families.

We heard stories about how she considered her secretaries her "confidantes" because she recognized the value of the relationship, the work they did together, and the need for everyone to be part of a valued team.

When asked about any relationship post-divorce, she volunteered that some friends had tried to set her up. Once there was a double date with friends, the man was nice but "no chemistry." She said it wasn't for lack of trying on her friends' parts because they thought it would be nice. When asked if she was lonely either as a professional or personally. Her reply was **I wasn't lonely on the job. Too busy to be lonely. Weekends were restful or going to basketball games or soccer games or getting involved in kid activities or just reading. No. I don't think I was lonely. I certainly wasn't lonely for a man, that's for sure.** (4th interview, March 7, 2023).

When she was at Central, she **spent time chatting with teachers in the hallways during passing time, connecting mostly with people as**

much as I could during the day. I'd walk the building a lot, checking on kids, checking on the elevator (She chuckled at this because the elevator was designed for those who needed it, not for those who were lazy about climbing stairs so one always had to monitor it.) Because she was out and about, she was out of her office, often not carrying her radio. When people needed to find her, word would circulate about where there was a "Mackbee sighting" and someone would go get her, if necessary.

Mary believed that to honor people and build community, it was important to celebrate—holidays, birthdays, weddings, divorces, beginning and ending of school years, just about any excuse was a good one. Plus, she believed that when something was worthy of celebrating, it was worthy of making it special which meant having tablecloths, flowers on the table, and room for people to sit talk and eat together. If was important that everyone was included For example, when they would have potlucks for lunches, she made sure that not all the food was put out for the first two lunches, and that there was enough for those who had third lunch. An ongoing specialty of hers for these events, which was requested and expected was Mary's famous for homemade bread pudding with brandy/butter sauce. (She claimed the alcohol cooked out of it.)

Her belief in the value of people was evident when she was supposedly DEmoted, she reframed it as being PROmoted to principal of Central High School, because she said that was her best job because she could be with kids. They remained her prime focus all the years she was there. The entire staff in the building were charged with educating kids in the best possible way.

Fairness

Fairness implies, and infers, doing the right thing for the right reason. It does not mean that everyone gets what they want or that everyone gets exactly the same thing. For education it rests on the belief in the value of the Common Good which is greatly ignored in our society today. An underpinning of public education in the United States is that we teach and do what supports the Common Good, the benefit for society in general, not for each specific person uniquely. However, we have become invested in "me", what's best for "me", forgetting that "me" is one, small part of humanity. Fairness also implies doing the right thing for the right reason, not necessarily the most political thing to do.

Mary practices fairness and doing the right thing for the right reason by her veritable nature. We have seen instances in her life story where she demanded fairness, like the time the District Office was going to cut millions from the secondary instruction budget but not from other departments and she demanded that other departments be cut as well. In doing this, Mary had stood up to the Superintendent and Finance Director which possibly led to her demotion from the District Office position of Director of Secondary

Teaching and Learning. No one else confronted the Superintendent or Finance Director.

As a building principal she often had to defend all the programs at Central because they had more diverse programs than other high schools which actually met the needs as they had a most diverse population than of the other high schools in St. Paul. In fairness, Mary believed in having programs that met the needs of all students from those in the Automotive Program to the Graphic Art program to the IB program to the Child Care opportunity in the building. Central also had one of the highest graduation rates in the state which should reinforce the recognition to people that student needs were being met and that, by and in itself, should be supported.

Fairness was even a consideration when Mary made sure there was enough potluck lunch for the people with the third lunch. She was aware of what was going on.

Fair does not imply equal. For example, some people may need less instruction in a certain topic; others need more. If the goal is for knowledge or mastery, then it is necessary to give to each what they need. The end result must be kept in mind.

It was not even fair that Central was scrutinized more heavily by the media and police because of the supposed involvement of Black students. If there was ever an incident, that had perhaps gone out on the radio because various agencies and newspapers monitor police scanners for example, suddenly the media would be on the sidewalks trying to talk to students. Other schools did not have that level of scrutiny which was racist in focus. Nor did Central get the same level of attention for positive results such as the Blue Ribbon Award, successful graduates, high graduation rates.

For example, St. Paul Central was named as a Blue Ribbon School of Excellence in 1997-98. As part of the award the school is welcome to post a banner on the outside of the school for five years recognizing this award. It is very unusual for an inner-city high school to earn this award, particularly at the time it was given. The award parameters have changed now, and they are not as encompassing to total programming. When Central received this award, the newspapers and Mayor were all notified of the day of celebration that we were hosting. It was a big deal. NO public official or media outlet showed up. I guess it was not a 911 call.

Mary demanded equal pay for equal work when her colleague was hired for the same job but put on a salary scale two steps higher than she. When confronted by this, the Superintendent changed her pay level to be the same.

When Mary was principal of Central and in principal meetings, other principals felt that Central had everything—Gifted/Talented programs, auto, the arts, technology programs, Black Box theater, and so on—and they did not have all the same programs. They also did not have the same needs as diverse Central. It was fair to provide students with what they need. Each school needed to have programs designed for their students.

Justice

Justice is a "kissing cousin" of fairness which means being just implies being fair, that the needs are addressed in a manner commiserate with the needs; that the rewards are commensurate with the level of accomplishment, that justice may be fair but not equal.

Decisions with disciplinary issues is a place where justice is key. Hard and fast rules are meant to be guidelines, but human considerations must be considered. Mary was keen on enforcing rules, but she was also keen on recognizing that discipline must be just and a learning experience.

As a young woman Mary fought for racial justice when she was involved in a "kneel in" in an all-white Catholic church in Selma. She continued to fight for racial justice in her administration of Central.

Listener and being non-judgmental

With her belief in people and her desire to create community, Mary was, and is, a great listener. Her door was always open to everyone (although sometimes she was not in the office but out in the halls). She also did a lot of "one-legged" listening, a phrase that means one is standing and someone comes up and says, "Have you got a minute?" That is a signal that this will take much longer than a minute, often several, so one stands on one leg and then the other. But she listens.

Mary has a friend who has opinions that are quite different from hers. The friend is much more critical of different ethnic groups and those who are perceived as less than worthy. Mary accepts the friend anyway because everyone has a right to their opinion, and Mary will try to ask questions to perhaps stimulate different ideas.

Because she is non-judgmental, she also does not carry grudges. Her experience with Curman Gaines is an example. He was a friend, then a boss, then mistreated her, and then tried to make amends. Mary was angry and hurt but was never bitter and can look at it now from a distance without any anger.

She is able to practice being non-judgmental in a way that keeps her from being angry about even racial slights and injustice. For example, when the father who was not used to dealing with Black teachers told her she had "pretty teeth, she **thought that was a compliment, I think. I didn't jump at people when they said things like that. I realize it's from a source of ignorance. I didn't say much, to him, just "thank you."** (2nd interview, February 8, 2023)

She demonstrates the ability to listen to many viewpoints, often in opposition to one another. **I think it's part of my natural style getting both sides of the picture. There's truth on the left side, truth on the right side. And then the real truth is right in the middle. You've got to have it all to really get at the real issue or the truth. That is especially true** with kids. They hold their own truth. With parents I think I was very diplomatic, which is part of my skill. Listening is part of that skill, not pushing people off because of their opinions, but listening and then make a decision based on what I wanted or what I thought was best. When I listen, I try not to judge. That's why I can still have breakfast with my friend with whom I disagree because I see the glass half full, and she sees it as half empty. When she pipes up with some of her stuff, I tell her it's a little racist. She knows she's judgmental, but in her defense, she is a really good teacher, great friend, and she did a lot of things for the school. (2nd interview, February 8, 2023)

Intelligent

Often in education people use their educational degrees as a pedigree to prove they are intelligent and credible. Mary does not need to prove she is intelligent by listing her degrees or her training.

A sign of innate intelligence is the ability to think for one's self. Mary did things that no one else did in her family or in her neighborhood. She went to a camp in upstate New York as a counselor when she had never done anything like that. She traveled to Washington D.C. alone during a time of civil unrest to attend a conference. She went to a student leadership conference in Madison, Wisconsin, the white North, when her experience was in the segregated South while still in high school.

She taught kindergartners during the summer in Selma, Alabama, right after the march from Selma to Montgomery, a time and place of heightened tensions and actions.

Why did she do these things? She had said she often felt like she was dropped into her family because she was doing these things and the others were not. She moved to Minnesota away from her family to a culture that was entirely new. They still live in Louisiana and she is in the "frozen North" without them although she has her own family now.

She taught classes through our universities on how to be an effective administrator. She has mentored many administrators, male and female, to help them in their positions. She has led a licensing board for educators statewide as they try to earn their licenses. She reads. She listens. All signs of an intelligent person.

Sense of Humor

Mary has an easy laugh and is willing to point fingers at herself when necessary. With this sense of humor comes a sense of humility. It's almost impossible for someone to have done what she has done if she did not find humor in humanity and with herself in particular.

Humility

Mary never brags about herself or her accomplishments because she does not feel the need to showcase what she knows or has done. In fact, when acknowledged for her efforts, she accepts the praise with great humility, in fact, often pointing out that the effort was the work of many.

An example is when asked about being the subject of this book, she hesitated. She did not want other people "bothered." When it was decided it would be her story in her words from her mouth, she finally agreed.

A prime example of her selflessness which is part of humility, Mary kept giving away her computers at school. She was one of the administrators who was out and about, engaging with students and staff. She did not lead from behind a computer screen. Actually, as computers became more and more a part of her job, she was not as skilled with the nuances of programs as others. She was capable but relied on secretaries and assistants to do a lot of the time-consuming things such as scheduling, spreadsheets, and so on. They could do it with greater ease and less time.

When the district would replace and upgrade computers, principals would get new machines. Mary's often sat relatively unused on her desk until someone, often a teacher, would come to her office and complain about their computer not working or not being upgraded. Typical Mary, "Here, take mine." And they would. She felt they needed it more than she did.

Generous

Mary will share whatever she has if you need it. That may be an offshoot of being raised in a large family who did not have a lot of stuff but there was a great need to support one another and share. She shares her house, time, and money with her family when they need it.

Plus, kids would come to her office and many times they were heard to say, "Ms. Mackbee, I don't have money for a prom dress. Ms. Mackbee, I can't afford a yearbook, Ms. Mackbee I......" Mary's response, "Here..." She never expected to be repaid and no one knew if she ever was. It did not matter.

She shares her time too. She is a great friend and takes care of people she loves. If she has a friend in a care facility, she visits often, takes people shopping, brings groceries, all the things one does to help.

Ethical

Mary Mackbee is known for doing the right thing for the right reason, politics aside. She believes in the Common Good, which some would say is a modern oxymoron. In the past schools were supposed to teach curriculum that would present several sides of topics with the goal of producing educated participatory citizens. Things now have become so polarized we have governors who decide that parts of AP courses cannot be taught in their state or that certain issues around sexuality cannot be mentioned in some classrooms. This is not the Common Good.

Mary's guiding principle is What Is right and best for kids? She used to fight to keep funding for the programs for all kids at Central and to keep class sizes down so teachers can teach to all kids.

She could be political in making decisions but she did not "play" politics. A good example is when she challenged the Superintendent and Finance Director over large cuts to secondary curriculum because it was not a cut across all areas and, hence, not fair. It also was not very political in that she challenged the Finance Director and Superintendent which may have led to her Demotion. But she was doing what she felt was right.

A Fighter

Mary had five brothers. She learned she had to fight for herself and for those she cared about. Remember when she fought the boys who were going to take Joe's bike? She fought the District Office over budget cuts, over unequal pay for the same job, and for the ability to use sick leave instead of unpaid leave for maternity time off. These are just some of the things she accomplished.

Another interesting story was about a female superintendent in St. Paul who thought it was an innovative idea to rate individual schools, in effect, pitting them against each other. **That turned out bad because those schools** [who received low ratings] **never regrouped because she labeled them as low performing. Plus, she said she was going to pick staff, her assistant superintendents from people she judged as champions of children. As though we all weren't. She picked. I was not chosen. I said, "I guess the rest of us aren't champions. We're all just

contenders. So I put that on my door. MARY MACKBEE, CONTENDER. (1ST interview, January 31, 2023)

At another time a fellow principal tried to take the Quest program to his school. **He worked behind my back with certain teachers to come to his school. I called Curman** [superintendent]. **He negated the teachers' transfers and they had to come back to Central. That principal was a "stinker." So were those teachers because they went behind my back, partly because they thought they could circumvent a female principal. It was a betrayal from the other principal and from the teachers** which offended Mary's strong sense of fairness. **The "stinker" principal was trying to build his program by taking my good teachers. He even took my science teacher because teachers could switch.** (2nd interview, February 8, 2023)

Problem-Solver

Mary prided herself on the fact that she made decisions. She was known for that skill. Interestingly in one of the graduate classes at the University, a professor suggested a strategy to deal with complex issues that needed a tricky decision of appointing a task force of more people engage with the issue and make a recommendation which gave the impression of dealing with it but, in actuality, slowed the process until sometimes the issue self-resolved or became a moot point. Sometimes, however, the problem got worse because individuals or groups acted out their own decisions, rarely cohesive ones. Delaying a decision was definitely not Mary's style.

Mary would absolutely gather the opinion of others. **I think my best guiding principle is that I am I real good problem-solver. I get ready. When something happens, I immediately go to, 'What do I need to do? How do I solve it?' I do that in my personal life too. I wonder, "How am I going to sell this?' My decisions have a lot of common sense because of experiences, life experiences.**

Part of being an effective problem-solver is knowing when a decision must be made, and it is not satisfactory to wait or postpone the decision. Sometimes a group is helpful to offer more opinions in the process and sometimes the leader must decide.

There usually has to be a resolution, otherwise it just hangs out there and can cause trouble.

An element of being a good problem-soler is having a system and routines so that people know how one operates and what procedures are in place. Those procedures can be the solution to an issue by themselves.

I like routines. For example, I always got to work around 6:30, had coffee, read the paper, went to the breakfast cafeteria, greeted the kids when they came in, walked the halls, rode the elevator, checked

the classrooms. If I had appointments, I'd be in my office. I was there. I was present. I was rarely absent from school. In fact, when I retired I had accumulated 400 sick days.

I tried to model the behavior that I hoped to get from others. I was the first one to say we don't need a staff meeting this month, so we would not have one. Just because a meeting is one the calendar, does not mean we have to have one, if there is no business.

However, I would call special meetings if an issue arose that everyone needed to know about. (4th interview, March 7, 2023)

I was born under the sign of Gemini—my personality can shift depending on the need. I'm comfortable in all situations—I can be in a house with a dirt floor and I'm comfortable. I can be in a house with Picassos and I make myself comfortable. I mean I'm not *as* comfortable, but I know which fork to use. (W-H, p. 124)

Conclusion

Mary has many assets: listening, fairness, non-judgmental, problem-solving, just, can be a fighter, humility, ethical, generous, and intelligence which are some of the skills she used every day as a parent, teacher, and administrator.

CHAPTER SEVEN

Leadership

The previous chapters probed the developmental foundation for Mary's leadership style.

The next step in understanding what made her so successful and enabling others to learn from her, we must hear Mary's definition of leadership and explore the concept of leadership in terms of sexism, racism, abstract leadership theories, and practical leadership in action.

Sexism

Sexism is not unique to the United States; it's international.

According to Gillard and Okonjo-Iweala in their book <u>Women and Leadership,</u> no women have ever led the United Nations or World Bank. In the United States, France, Nigeria, Mexico, or Japan, no woman has ever been president. Only fifty-seven nations of the 193 nations in the United Nations have ever had a woman hold their highest position. (p. 19) In an analysis of many international agencies this means that three out of every four political-decision makers in 2020 are men. In addition, "only 24% of persons heard, read about or seen in the news media are women. Even worse, only 4% of news stories clearly challenge gender stereotypes." (p. 23)

The inequity is visible in movies, sports, novels, and even Nobel Prize winners. Although women are the largest consumers of books, only fifteen women have been given the Nobel Prize for Literature in contrast to 101 men. Plus, we know that women currently write many books even though at one time, women, to be published, had to write under a male pseudonym, e.g., Amantine Lucile Aurore Dupin became George Sand, the Bronte sisters became the brothers Bell, and Mary Ann Elliot became George Eliot. In practical science applications, even the dummies used to test seat belts are made for the male physique. (p. 24) Professional female athletes still struggle to get comparable salaries to their male professional colleagues, such as in soccer.

Historically, our leaders have been white males, thereby creating a body of literature and acceptance of what a leader is supposed to be. According to Schwieger, et. al., "leadership theories reproduce romanticism by exaggerating the impact of individual leaders...which supports the heroic image of a leader. Such an emphasis avoids the complexities that comprise leadership because it oversimplifies the formulas for success. This leader-as-hero may be over-confident about their own abilities and may hinder their ability to be excellent in changing, uncertain conditions. Such heroic qualities serve as models for privileged masculine behavior making the prototypical leader a quintessentially masculine man." (Schweiger, p. 412-13)

"Gendered stereotypes of the heroic leader can lead to double-bind situations for both women and men. For women it creates a mismatch between qualities attributed to women and masculine qualities thought necessary for leadership. Men may find a paradox of two alternatives—reject traditional definitions of masculine behavior and risk being perceived as less of a man or they can embrace the hero definition of leader and pursue the task of having superman qualities. (Schweiger, P. 414)

Various stories and movies proliferate this idea of leaders as hero. For education, leaders-as-heroes are projected in such movies as <u>Lean on Me</u>, <u>Stand and Deliver.</u> A research article discovered in writing this book in the NASSP <u>Bulletin</u> in 1976, an article "Profile of a Principal—Blending Multiple Roles for Success" by Anne Marie Mistretta and Patricial Phillips. The principal was a white male who had his own homeroom, read a lot, spent time in the lunchroom and study hall, donated comfortable furniture to teachers' lounge, did Management by Walking Around, and was involved in a model curriculum program. The list goes on and on. He appeared to be capable of everything. It's interesting that two women helped perpetuate this idea of male superhero principal even in 1976.

The question arises do women and men lead differently? Plus, what's wrong, if anything, with the current models of leadership? Biologically, if one looks at the brain studies, scientists are not able to say that male and female brains are different in key areas. Brain size which is larger in men does not mean they are smarter; it just means that their larger, more muscular bodies need a larger brain. Studies have not been able to prove that higher levels of testosterone bathing a fetus in utero make a difference in whether a person will or will not have empathy. The idea that women are more understanding may be more a factor of socialization than biology.

Yet we see pop psychology selling the ideas of the so-called difference between men and women, e.g., books like <u>Men are from Mars; Women are from Venus.</u> We must be wary of "over-hyped news reports" that there is solid scientific evidence that sex differences are hardwired into our brains. (Gillard, p. 29)

Instead, what is more important is to "believe that to the extent that there are variations, they arise because, at every stage of life, men and women are socialized and stereotyped differently." (Gillard, p. 30) Are differences hard-wired:? Or just learned the hard way?

Therefore, it causes the discussion of whether women who are in leadership positions should try to act like a man in order to be seen as successful or should they examine how women have been socialized in a male-dominated society. How does this affect their leadership styles and practices? The discussion later in this book from Stacey Abrams in <u>Lead from the Outside</u> focuses on how to succeed in such a system.

It is intriguing that in conversations with women of the Gen Xers and GenYs, they have shared with this author that they do not always believe that sexism is still an issue for them because many of them, particularly the highly skilled women, have achieved successful careers. But the question remains, why has ERA never passed in all these years, why are we still debating the unequal medical rights of women, the discrepancy of salaries when women and men are in the same positions, the fact that that the Southern Baptist Church is voting to un-allow women pastors?

Education is one facet of this complicated culture of ours. Education has been, and still is, dominated by white men in positions of leadership. According to AASA, American Association of School Administrators, only 27% of superintendents are female, compared to 76% of the teaching staff. The number has increased only 2% in the last five years. In addition, in an article "Perceptions of Unconscious Gender Bias in the Superintendency: An Exploratory Quantitative Study" published in the Journal of Scholarship and Practice cited on the AASA website found in the largest study to date of 532 school district superintendents, there was compelling evidence that "unconscious gender bias exists on the job and further inhibits equitable representation in the superintendency." (AASA, 2023)

Scholarly studies of Black woman school superintendent are largely underrepresented in education leadership research and the field. (Oxford, 2023) Studies of other Black women administrators such as high school principals are even less common which is a tragedy because high school principals are often the feeders to superintendent positions. Research says that Black women are only 7% of the principals nationally. (Black women principals, April 20, 2023.)

For public high schools the statistics are even bleaker. "More specifically, Black women principals comprised about 4.8% of all principals in public secondary schools (making them unicorns among US secondary school principals." (NCES, 2009)   Black women often serve schools with higher percentages of students eligible for free and reduced lunch and a high percentage of students of color. It was also found that there was a positive association by teachers and female principals with the instructional leadership of these women. There was also a higher math achievement scores among students with female principals. (Educational Administration Quarterly, 2023)

In the qualitative study on <u>Self-Determinants of Success by the Women who are head Principals in High Schools in Minnesota</u> all twenty-six had experienced gender bias in determining their career choice or on the job. The study was completed in 1995 and some things have changed, we hope. However, several patterns are still present. For one, there are few role models, particularly for women of color. (There was only one principal of color in this study because there was only one such woman in the state at that time.) (Sigford, 1995)

In Minnesota there are 331 school districts currently. Of that 331, there are 6 Black female superintendents which is a little over 1%. However, at one time there were Black women as superintendents in both Minneapolis and St. Paul, and at the same time, Minneapolis had a Black female mayor. In school year 95-95 when Sigford did her study of head high school principals, there were six high schools in St. Paul; three were led by women, one by a Black woman—Mary Mackbee. There are now more high schools in St. Paul because of specialized programs, but only two have Black women principals. However, another school is led by a Hmong female. So percentage-wise it is not any further along than in 1994-95. Also, it is interesting that St. Paul now has a Black male mayor, Melvin Carter, who was a Central student during Mary's tenure as principal. He even spoke at her retirement party. Plus, she spoke at his first inauguration!

Racism

The next question is how does societal racism affect the socialization of our leaders who are people of color? Do people of color, particularly women, find it doubly hard to lead because of experienced racism and sexism? In her book Dr. Hynes described the workplace issue in that only 12% of black women are in positions of management, business, and financial operations. Sadly, 53% of black women are sole-income earners yet have a higher representation (28%) of those of earn income below the poverty level. (Hynes,p. 30)

"Oftentimes, the racial and sexual elements are downplayed in the work environment but there is sufficient evidence to support the combination of these two constructs creates the concrete wall." (p. 40) What is a reality for white women as the "glass ceiling"; for women of color, it has a double whammy creating a "concrete wall." (Hynes, p. 40) Stacey Abrams, the first Black woman to receive the nomination by a major political party as she ran for the governorship in Georgia, wrote a book entitled <u>Lead from the Outside</u> where she probes the issues of how to deal with racism and sexism as they create a culture of what she calls "outsiders" who seek leadership opportunities. More on this in the section on practical application.

The environment above is the environment in which Mary was socialized.

Mary's definition of Leadership

Everyone has their own definition of leadership. This is Mary's. **I don't have a one sentence definition. It's almost like a conditional definition, depending on the situation, depending on the problem. I guess you could say it's situational because on occasions I can be a dictator and just tell people what they have to do if that's important, or I can be a negotiator; I can be a compromiser; I can be a collaborator but with a lot of heart. I think heart over head is my philosophy because, I always say, in terms of facts, I do the best I can with what I have at the time, the information and then try not to second guess.** (5th interview, March 21, 2023)

I love to solve problems and I do it quickly without regret.

I can be a dictator if some people need it, for example, if there are teachers who don't provide lessons for kids and who try to teach from the seat of their pants. I have to get tough on people in terms of what responsibilities are, if they are too lackadaisical about kids not wanting to learn so they hold back in terms of their teaching.

When I was subbing as an administrator last week, I was walking by a class and the kids were all on their ipads. If I were an administrator there full-time, I'd have to call [the teacher] in and say, 'You know, the kids expect some interactive kinds of conversations, not just interacting on an ipad with some faceless screen or some kind of exercise.' I can be a dictator when it comes to classroom instruction and people not earning their keep, not doing right for kids.

She uses the metaphor of a push broom to describe her leadership style. Sometimes it cleans up, clears the way for others, and sometimes sweeps up behind them.

People get used to a single way and become comfortable in terms of their environment. The trick is for me to build the capacity within the staff and in the leadership, I leave behind. That's why I never see myself as the savior; it's the teachers who create the academic rigor in this building, and it's my other assistant principals and counselors who work with kids to help them succeed and get them into good colleges. I simply support all that. I don't see myself as being *the* force— Leadership is power.

I don't believe in a single source of power. Power is an expression of the power of people. Power is when the staff all have the same purpose and work towards it. And as a leader, one helps them define that purpose and gives them the resources they need to do that. But power is not a single person; it's a collective. The staff at Central had power; they could change things, influence things with me. Some changes I had implemented myself, but it takes a collection of people to really create power. Otherwise, you [the leader] don't have power.

Do men see power and the power of leadership differently? **Some of the men I've worked for have been more sensitive, a couple, not many. Some think they are in charge of the school, rather than the leader of the school. There's a difference. Some of delegated a lot and some were more figureheads. They would hire an assistant that really ran the school; I saw that a lot.** Mary is describing men who perform as the leaders-as-hero. **I can think of one who had a lot of heart. I think women prefer shared leadership; the majority of men just like to be in charge, more likely to dictate. There are a few that lead more like a woman, but that's few and far between. Most of them are just in power positions, making sure their voice is the one that's heard and followed, not wanting to share the "stage" with others.**

I think when people believe in your abilities, maybe that's power because then you can affect a lot of change. When I first got to Central, I followed a woman, who had been preceded by only men. I came under a cloud of being demoted from the District so I guess I had more to prove than the average principal. Once they got to know me and realized I was a fair person and had the interests of the teachers and kids at the heart of whatever you want to call my leadership, or power. Then I think they bought in.

It wasn't easy. Central was not an easy place, it was considered to be the inner-city school with all the inner-city problems. At that point it had the highest percentage of kids of color, mostly Black, highest percentage of Black kids at any high school in the city. It was located in a part of town where there's a lot of crime. But it had an excellent reputation. We had bright kids who came from outside of St. Paul, Stillwater, White Bear Lake, because of the academic programs.

We always had good teachers. When I got there, there were some who were a little weird and some who left because they weren't that good. They were in retirement mode already, so they didn't last once I got there because I put a little pressure on them because they were so ready for retirement.

I got the book <u>One Minute Manager.</u> Some of the things they say, like encourage staff. I do that. I'm not a manager of people I respect because I don't have to. They take care of themselves. I take them as they are and if there's some fault, we try to work on it.

There are some good teachers who had some issues with Black kids. I would say, 'You know, you have to deal with all the kids.' For a lot of them, when you pointed out that it was implicit bias, they weren't always aware. Sometimes I'd write them up and if they were on probation, they got marked down in terms of relationships, or equity issues with kids. Most of them, you'd encourage them to do some in-service training which the district had. I would also call in a specialist as a coach to do more coaching if I did not have time to coach. (2nd interview, February 8, 2023).

Mary's role models were black educators, men and women. Living in a Black community allowed her to see Black men and women in leadership positions. In fact, they inspired her to become an educator. They were dedicated professionals who lived in the community, went to the same church, shopped in the same stores.

Abstract definition of Leadership

Popular psychology has contributed book after book, article after article, about leadership. There are whole sections in bookstores designated just to this topic.

Scholarly research and dissertations have also contributed to the literature by using research techniques to analyze the topic. However, research examines what has already happened or what is currently happening but is not necessarily advisory, nor proscriptive. The hope is that others will learn and make inferences to incorporate into their own practice. However, the voice of the practitioners, as opposed to the voice of researchers, is not heard as often, unless the research is a qualitative study which is not as common because, one, in the academic world quantitative research is more prestigious and "scientific", and two, it's time-consuming and often difficult to get access to a cross-section of practitioners.

Over time the literature has been seen as showing that leadership falls into five major types which are:

- Authoritarian leadership (autocratic) ...
- Participative leadership (democratic) ...
- Delegative leadership (laissez-faire) ...
- Transactional leadership (managerial) ...
- Transformational leadership (visionary) (types, 2023)

In the authoritarian style, the leader makes decisions alone, apart from the group, and is seen as the final authority. The title alone now has negative connotations and may be associated with people like Hitler, Napoleon, presidents, and CEOs of some major companies. It is a style that is often thought of as the traditional viewpoint of leadership, and thought to be largely a male domain, perhaps even largely a white male domain. Not many people currently aspire to being this type of leader all the time;

however, there are times when the leader must decide, and it may not be the decision that the group would have made. But the leader has a wide-angle view of the organization, its needs, its people, its goals and others may not have the same information and needs to act.

There are definite pluses and minuses. On the plus side, decisions can be made quickly. People know who to go to for a decision. On the minus side, there may be little engagement or buy-in to the decision. Workers may feel disconnected.

Another style is the Participative Style which is democratic. Employees are involved in the process of making decisions, therefore having more information about the overall concerns, needs, and outlook. Employees may feel more valued, more a part of the organization.

However, on the downside, it may take longer to make decisions. Also, within group dynamics if some of the group feel one way and there is another viewpoint, those holding the opposing or minority viewpoint, may leave feeling discounted and unheard. This type of leadership takes someone with strong listening and group facilitation skills to manage it.

A third style is Delegative Leadership, which is seen when the leader gives the employees autonomy and creative freedom to perhaps set their own goals and schedules. On the plus side, employees experience great freedom and great individual responsibility. For self-motivated and directed individuals, this meets their needs. However, decisions that affect the whole group are often stalled, put aside, or ignored. Some employees may need direction and they are not able to perform at their best unless they know what is expected. One often associates this style with a more artistic temperament and enterprise. It is not effective in a large organization if that is the sole style that is used.

Managerial leadership is the type where a leader sets targets and procedures. It is different from the autocratic in that there can be some give-and-take with employees on decisions. There is some input from employees, but the manager sets the goals and targets. Some people function well under this type because it is common in today's organizations. Schools have often fallen into this category to a degree. As an institution either at a district or building level, the system may be managerial. Yet inside a classroom teachers may have more of the delegative style where they are in charge and are able to fulfill expectations and goals in their respective ways.

The fifth style is Visionary Leadership or transformational. This leader wants to energize a group to create something new, wanting employees to see new possibilities. Some people find this exciting. Others find it unsettling because they need parameters. This style may be trendy for an organization who wants something different, saying they want a visionary. Some leaders describe themselves as such. However, being truly visionary is not the same as doing the same thing in a different way. For example, it is not necessarily visionary to go from a six-period day to a seven-period day because it's been done before and is more of a managerial procedure that may meet the current needs of the organization. Being truly visionary is difficult because often one is going away from what is known and what has been done before, which is difficult and threatening to some.

Mary Mackbee's own practice of leadership incorporates all five, with the authoritative style used sparingly. She can be a manager, when necessary, but does enjoy participatory leadership. She has been visionary in incorporating new programs into the high school, as well. She uses the delegative style when she utilizes others' expertise to let them do what they do best, plus when she is mentoring upcoming administrators to get experience in different situations. Any good leader probably incorporates pieces of all styles depending on the needs of the organization and situation. It's true that different organizational cultures demand different styles and outcomes. In educational settings different buildings in the same district may demand different leadership styles because buildings have different cultures and different needs from each other. The trick is to know when to use what and when to stop using something that worked somewhere else but does not work in the new situation.

Knowing about such leadership styles is only one facet of leadership. The next step, an important one but one that is often not considered, is to look at the person as leader and to match style with the needs of the organization. Not every person can be slotted into any leadership position and be successful. Therefore, it is important to know the person, their beliefs, principles, values because we lead who we are.

For the purposes of this book, it was difficult to find qualitative studies of women leaders, particularly women high school principals, to hear their voices about their leadership in action. It was even more difficult to find studies of Black women leaders.

However, we do have the advantage of a study of women superintendents done by Dr. C. Cryss Brunner, Professor Emerita of the University of Minnesota. When she was an Assistant Professor of Educational Administration at the University of Wisconsin-Madison, she studied women superintendents and wrote her book <u>Principles of Power: Women Superintendents and the Riddle of the Heart.</u> Although the study is with superintendents and other district level administrators, it is from the principal ranks that these jobs are usually filled. Therefore, the insights gained from studying the leadership issues of superintendents can be applied to such positions as high school principal, such as Mary Mackbee's relevant experiences.

C.Cryss Brunner's Research

Her book chose to use metaphor to downplay what she called "culturally coercive" behavior that has idealized male behavior.

Research studies of leadership have largely been reductionistic by describing behaviors and actions within the leadership setting, ignoring the personal factors that have led to the person in the role. However, a leader and leadership are a composite of many factors which, no matter what is read, or what training is received, how the ideas will be used is not prescriptive. Leadership comes down to the person; it cannot be separated from the person in the role.

As stated above, the research on Black men and women in the role of leader is scant.

However, for the purpose of this book, the women listed in Brunner's study are almost entirely white females. Once again, the Black leader's voice is a whisper. However, this particular book will add the voice of Mary Mackbee to the discussion as an example of a successful Black leader in public education. All that being said, Brunner's study should be replicated using the voices of Black women and other women of color to see what, if anything, is different,

In Brunner's study she discovered that the women superintendents find that the structure of governance which is "one of authority or control" does not facilitate what they perceived as the current educational challenges: 1) administering schools to improve academic performance of students, 2) addressing social problems through schools, 3) rethinking organizational structures that may not be able to address the above concerns." (Brunner, p. 29)

The top concerns of the women were in two areas: "1) relationships in general, and most important, 2) the well-being, both academically and generally, of the children." (Brunner, p. 33) The concerns of male superintendents rest more in the area of management—financial, procedural-- which does not imply that male superintendents do not care, or that women do not take care of the necessary managerial tasks. It suggests that women have been socialized to pay attention to the personal values stressing relationships and men have learned to focus on management and control.

Brunner extrapolated five principles that were made evident by the women in the study.

First Principle: Knowing the Battleground

The superintendency or principalship is a position of power. The first principle in looking at power is stated as "knowing the battleground" which means it is crucial for the leader to know what is expected, to know the culture, and to know what performance tasks are necessary for success, such as managing the budget, and ways to communicate in a masculinized culture, Women have named the strategies they have learned to work around as: 1) being silenced by the term *power,* 2) overt silencing; 3) listening as different than silence; and 4) ways to communicate to be heard.

Overt silencing happens by such tactics as people physically turning away as someone is speaking, or by merely not listening by paying attention to someone else, or by engaging on a cell phone during an in-person conversation, or when men dominate and monologue the conversation to a point where a woman cannot interject. A frequent communication problem is that men tend to interrupt rather than wait for a woman to finish her thought as though their ideas are more important. Also, women report the need to hide their emotions in order to be seen as credible. In some trainings a trainer has been known to say, "never cry."

Another circumstance is if a woman is with a man, another speaker addresses the man, ignoring the woman, regardless of position, or topic. Often, for women superintendents because they are relatively rare, it is assumed that a man is the superintendent. People will be surprised that the leader is female. Many of these tactics could be described not only as overt silencing, but also as overt sexism.

When one adds the added dimension of race to this discussion, the overt silencing becomes even greater. Racism and sexism combine to silence.

When asked if Mary had to change her communication patterns as she dealt with the men in the district, she said, **sometimes a woman would speak, but a man would blurt something out in the middle of the talk and expect women to listen. I had many problems at meetings. I felt I wasn't being heard because they just kind of ignored my comments. I'd say something profound, I thought, and they would just ignore my comments. Then another very domineering principal would say the** exact same thing, and it was all praise and glory, you know. But I was always outspoken. I was a rebel. I fought the district a lot on things when they tried to change the schedule or get rid of the Quest program.

By fighting she meant, **I spoke up. I think that's why my colleague and I were demoted because we didn't kowtow to Curman** [the superintendent]. **When he said it was my job to make him look good, I said that wasn't my job.**

Did she find it true that men tended to talk over her? **Absolutely, or ignore me. Even turn away and start talking to somebody else when you're talking to them. It happened when I was a principal and when I was a director. I remember at a budget meeting one time, and I was just livid because they were going to cut 35 million – a lot—out of our budget. I told them if they cut it from my budget, they should also cut from somebody else's.**

I guess I grew up in the kind of environment where one listens to all the facts before making a decision, no turning back. It's like they always say, I made the best decision that I could with the information I had at the time. So that was my motto. If I learn something else later, well, too late. The decision was made.

Was she able to be heard when she would speak up? **It was a fight at the principals' meetings. I remember it was always a struggle because of the guys, I don't know if they were insensitive or just** pompous. It was also their relationship with the women in their own lives too, I think, that permeated some of how they dealt with women at work. I don't think a lot of them had strong women at home. If they did, the women ran the household. I remember one of the most vocal and domineering man at the meetings, his wife could make him do anything at home. I remember going there one time because we were doing negotiations. We had a meeting at his house; she put us in the basement for the meeting, nearly froze my ass to death because it was freezing. I had to keep my coat on the whole time. She put us downstairs because she was not comfortable with him working with women. So too with another colleague's wife. When I was an assistant principal, his wife would come over at lunch time to make sure he wasn't going out to lunch with me. He had told the Assistant Superintendent that his wife did not want her husband working with a female A.P. We later found out she was mentally ill and did some strange things.

Was this rude behavior because you were female or was it because you were Black?

There were a lot of Black kids at that school and a few Black staff. But at the high school it was mostly about being female, rather than about being Black. This is reminiscent of what Shirley Chisholm found to be true too, that she was ignored more because she was female, than because she was Black.

At the District Office the rude behavior was more about trying to one up one another and just tons and tons of meetings. You get so tired of them. [the men who do this.]

The second communication challenge was *listening as different from silence*. Most of the women in Brunner's study found they did not talk as much as they would have liked because they wanted to be seen as respectful and gaining information. Consequently, they often stayed silent. (Brunner, p. 47) It is necessary to listen to gain information. However, when women feel almost forced to be silent, it is not respectful. There are vestiges of the old belief that men should be heard and women, to be respectful and "nice', should be quiet.

The women in the study acknowledged the need to be a listener. But being a good listener is respectful and helps build relationships, if it is not done at the expense of getting heard.

Mary Mackbee is an excellent listener. As we heard earlier, she maintained an open door to students, parents, staff, colleagues. Her goal of creating a family among the staff and developing strong relationships in the community depended upon her listening. Her innate talent for being non-judgmental played a strong role in her being a productive listener to really hear what was being said. It also contributed to one of her greatest strengths of being a good problem-solver. One cannot solve problems effectively if one does not know all the many sides of an issue.

A third communication challenge is *how to develop strategies to be heard*. Throughout conversations it became apparent that there were six strategies women developed: 1) not being direct, 2) using spokespersons; 3). Careful use of language; 4) timing, 5) stepping around egos, and 6) preparation.

One of the ways women have developed to not be direct is to state things in a passive voice because being too direct is seen as too aggressive or assertive. Instead of "I thought…" or "That's not a good idea," one asks questions, "What would happen if?", "Would it be better if we…." Asking questions softens the viewpoint and asks for input. Another way to not be direct and, is an affectation this author hears on television, on podcasts, in speeches, is when women end a sentence by raising the pitch of the voice. The voice goes up, instead of down, as it normally would at the sentence as though one were asking a question. Again, that makes it seem that the comment is not a statement of fact, but more like a question, and not assertive.

Using spokespersons is another communication strategy. Quoting a so-called expert, or repeating what someone else said, or citing research are techniques to have someone else be the expert, to validate the woman's ideas.

Another strategy is to *be careful about the use of language.* One must be careful of not using too many typically female examples, perhaps not using family, particularly one's children, as an example. Another one is the use of swear words. Many people feel that is inappropriate at any time but there is a reason some people call it "locker room talk" because people associate it with sports, particularly male sports. Women also need to avoid speech interrupters like the word, "like" which is another affectation. One seldom hears a man using that speech pattern.

The timing of conversations is strategic. Making certain that the group is ready to hear. Sometimes it takes repeating an idea, perhaps in more than one way or in more than one meeting.

Some administrators talked about stepping around egos, meaning they felt the need to "dumb down" what she knew in her presentation so she would not come across as the "expert" to the point that several women who have advanced degrees felt the need to downplay that education.

Preparation is the last strategy Brunner mentioned. Obviously, it is wise to be always prepared. Sometimes women felt like they over-prepared to be ready for any questions or comments. They did not feel they had the freedom to say, "I don't know" because that made them seen as less credible.

Authority is often assumed when one hears a loud voice or a is listening to large person. Men have louder voices and are usually larger than women. Men have, and use, their bodies to communicate power and leadership. As a small woman, Mary was not afraid of using her voice to be heard, regardless of her size. Remember, she had five brothers, all bigger than she.

Mary Mackbee felt the need to use these strategies in communication. Several things worked in her favor. One, she was raised with five brothers, which made her more assertive. She was not intimidated by a group of men. She was willing to state her viewpoint, maybe more than once if she was fighting for something. Another advantage was the respect she had among her peers. Mary had worked in the district for many years in many capacities, so longevity gave her an advantage in that she knew the "players" and they knew her. As she said, she knew where all the bodies were buried, particularly after having worked at the District Office. Another advantage for Mary as a Black woman may have been that she had been part of white Minnesota for so long she was able to navigate the culture. She had learned the "hidden rules." As time progressed throughout her tenure in St. Paul, more voices from people of color were at the table which was an advantage as well.

If an administrator comes into a new situation, she is more likely to use various communication strategies. As a seasoned member of the group, Mary had to learn which strategies worked and which did not.

Second Principle: Discarding the Unnecessary

The job of administrator is time-consuming. To be successful, one must learn to concentrate on what is important and to eschew that which is not. Time management is key. Resource management is required, which means eliminating things that keep one from accomplishing the goals.

Women in the study spoke of having to give up certain things to focus. The things they had to give up were: 1) intimate relationships, 2) friendships, 3) privacy, and 4) myths.

Many of the women who were in Brunner's study were from the era of being socialized in the 50s and 60s and the gender roles of the time. The two-person career household was less common. At that point wives were to maintain households and entertain guests including the husband's work colleagues. It was also perceived by male school boards that women could not handle the time and professional demands of a superintendency because of commitments at home.

Things have changed, somewhat. Two career families are common; however, studies show that women still do more household chores than men and that men have more leisure time than women. Women make most of the decisions about household décor in 62% of households. They are also more likely to care for the children daily, shop for groceries, and wash dishes. Men still do the lion's share of things like car maintenance, and yard work.

(Guardian, 2022). Many educational administrators have had to negotiate through "role conflict." in how they spend their time.

We still see this role conflict played out nationally. Not too long-ago Hillary Clinton ran for President with speculation circulating as to even what her husband, Bill, would be called. It played out again when Kamala Harris became Vice President. What would her husband, Doug Emhoff, be called? He is the "second gentleman", the first in history. Then there was public debate about how he would handle his career. He put his career on hold during her tenure. Not everyone can or will do that.

A parallel discussion was what would happen to Dr. Jill Biden, an educator, if her husband, Joe Biden became President because she was a working wife. She continues to teach English and writing at Northern Virginia Community College which is where she taught before the election. Both Doug Emhoff and Jill Biden were "role breakers", changing the norms. There are a multitude of solutions to the dilemma of gender roles, who does what and when, who gets advanced degrees, who works full or part-time as there are working couples, particularly those with children. They have reported that men find it harder to change their role responsibilities. (Brunner, p. 62) Sometimes it does not work; many women in administrative roles are single or divorced, often becoming single mothers which becomes another struggle and management issue by itself.

However, children still often rest in the woman's domain. The father may be a strong partner, but often takes parenting suggestions at the direction of the mother. (I do not think the same dilemma is over car maintenance.) Smile!!

Women often enter administration later than men, after children are older.
The age of children does not usually enter a that decision for a man. Consequently, women are often older when entering this part of their career, also having usually spent more time in a classroom as a teacher.

Mary Mackbee is a living example of this issue. First, she had received a very traditional message from her Catholic upbringing that if you had sex, you should be married. She married Earsell Mackbee. She started as a two-career family, and ended up being a single mother, raising four children, including taking care of a disabled adult child, all without help from her ex-husband.

Mary supported the household, including making the mortgage payment. She even paid for Earsell's car. She had childcare expenses, initially, on a teacher's salary.

After nineteen years Mary filed for divorce, making Mary a de facto single mother, even though she had been functioning as one for years. She said it had felt like at that time, she had five, not four, children.

As the children got older and she was an administrator with many evening commitments, she felt bad that she was not home as much as she would like. However, her response to your kids if they complained was that "Do you want food? Transportation? Clothes"? Looking back, she thought they probably thought she was not home as much as they would have liked, but she was at their sporting and dance events, and provided a home. Now as adults they can recognize the effort that was taken because they too are adults facing some of the same issues.

When asked how she did all that, she said she really did not know but that you do what you must do. No sense feeling sorry for oneself; just do it.

Friendships

Women have reported that it is difficult to maintain relationships. Work takes many hours; personal care, home, and children maintenance take many hours. What's left? One needs time to relax, perhaps even read, which leaves little time for maintaining friendships.

In spite of that Mary was able to be part of a women's support group in her district with other female administrators and has maintained several strong friendships with these women today. It has not always been easy to do so.

Privacy

Administrators give up a certain amount of privacy. The administrator is a notable person in the community. Women have felt doubly scrutinized as communities make judgments about appearance, possible friendships, whether someone goes to church or not, where one socializes whether it's a bar or restaurant.

Women feel their behavior needs to be above reproach. Unmarried women are subjected to even greater scrutiny which is even more pronounced in smaller communities where it is difficult to do anything anonymously. In such communities, women may drive to another town to shop or go out. It is somewhat easier in a larger metropolitan area.

In some communities it is hoped that a superintendent will live in the district which demonstrates to the community that the superintendent is truly committed. The same is true with other administrators, including principals. Community members like seeing their school officials living and working and playing in the community. Mary remembers her admired administrators being a part of her community in the Seventh Ward.

Mary talked earlier about how living in Bloomington helped. Her kids went to different schools than the ones she led; she shopped in different places than where she worked. However, she spent a lot of time in St. Paul. She was at school events, Gospel choir concerts, and other community events. She was a recognized community in the Central community, maybe even more than in Bloomington but the physical separation helped her to recharge on weekends.

Discarding Myth

There is a certain expectation, or myth, about how a woman executive should appear and act, based on the premise that male past practice is the standard. Women were advised to dress in a certain way and "never cry." We discussed this earlier about how Mary dressed conservatively, not provocatively feminine. She dressed in clothes that allowed her to walk the halls, to interfere in altercations, and yet, appear well-groomed in meetings. Plus, Mary wore black and red a lot in various combinations of sweaters, jackets, vests, suits to honor the school colors of Central.

Black women have been criticized in the past for hair styles that are natural or afro. Hopefully, that is fading. Women have been criticized if their clothes are bright colors. Hopefully, that is fading as well because we can all use a little color in our lives. Men have been known to be impatient when two women talk of manicures, pedicures, or even childcare issues; however, in contrast women do not have the luxury of being impatient about Monday morning rehash of every week-end football game and sometimes they learn to "talk football" or to learn the game so they can participate. Trust me, it can be painful to spend an hour each Monday morning at team meetings replaying football.

It's sometimes a fine line between maintaining a sense of femininity, not playing into overtly feminine behaviors or conversations, and yet not "acting like a man."

Sexual innuendos

Occasionally, someone will still comment that a woman "slept her way to the top". Mary dealt with this when she was asked to become part of the District Office team. If a male administrator is known to have had relationships with some female staff, others wonder if any woman who works with him is also sleeping with him. There were even rumors that wondered if she and her colleague were sleeping together because they worked so closely. Men and women can be friends without being sexually involved.

Plus, there is the insecurity with some wives if their husband works closely with a woman, particularly if she is attractive. Remember the fishing week-end story of Mary? The men had a traditional fishing weekend and a female teacher wanted to join, asking Mary to come as well. When they signed up, the event was soon cancelled. Why? The wives put a stop to it with the excuse that the cabin did not have privacy and accommodation for both sexes. There was the previous example where a wife showed up at school at lunch to make certain Mary was not with the woman's husband. Evening meetings are another time when wives call or set up conflicting events with the meeting to check that nothing is going on.

Another difficult time for women is when they are a singleton at an event, a dinner, a banquet, when everyone else is coupled. Unless she knows one or more of the wives, conversations can be difficult. It takes a confident woman to meander through dinner, perhaps dancing.

The off-color jokes have diminished in the workplace in the last several years partly because of #MeToo. It's a relief.

Principle Three: Choosing Battles

Women administrators were consciously aware of carefully choosing their battles. In starting a new position, it is incumbent upon them to listen because women must prove themselves. New male superintendents do as well, but, if someone is the first female in the position, people are watching. One will seldom see two female superintendents hired in succession in a district. No one flinches if two, or more, men are hired in a row. In fact, that is taken as the norm.

Superintendent search firms will often bring forward a token female or a token person of color (It's sometimes the same person) when districts are looking to hire. Women of color are looked at seriously if a district has had an overt issue with racism or if the population is suddenly changing. Women of color are more likely to be hired in urban settings, charter schools, or specialized schools.

Therefore, if becomes necessary for her success for any female administrator, superintendent, principal, or district office, to examine the culture, listen, and then choose their focus or "choose their battles."

Overwhelmingly, women will say that their primary concern is the students. Men in conversation focus on finance, transportation, and facilities. School board meetings focus on the same issues, not on curriculum. Men seldom talk about curriculum in fact, in this current political climate post-COVID, curriculum and professional development have taken a back seat to the idea of surviving and doing the best people can. Discussions about curriculum have been replaced about how and when to use tablets and other technological choices to deliver education. However, test scores have taken a hit because we as educators know that learning and teaching is a very human, interactive process. Putting a worksheet on a screen is still a worksheet. The art of group work, discussion, and human interactions has been severely damaged during COVID, as witnessed by the increase in mental health issues, discipline issues with students, and teacher burn-out. Administrators and teachers alike have felt that the last three years have made everyone 'pick their battles" which has put them in a stressful survival mode.

Post-retirement Mary has subbed as an administrator in some buildings in St. Paul. She has witnessed the difference in student behavior from post-COVID. **In middle school when telling kids to get to class,**

kids say they do not have to go until high school when credits matter. I guess the best thing yesterday with a kid who never went to class is that he used to cuss me out. Now he just ignores me. He moves but he won't go to class. If in class, they are so disruptive or dysfunctional, one cannot teach. The kids don't have good reading or writing skills or socialization skills because they are on the screen all the time shooting at things. It's selfishness. They want what they want. Adults want them in class; but they don't want to be there. (1st interview, January 31, 2023)

Principle Four: Taking Risks

Brunner examined research studies about superintendents as risk takers. Did districts want someone who takes risks? Did search firms look for that in candidates? What she found is that school administrators have never been portrayed as risk takers. Risk-taking was not among the fifty-two skills identified under eight performance areas identified as skills expected of administrative candidates. (Brunner, p. 83) Instead, administrators look for ways to make their organizations more effective. They try to succeed within the budget parameters, achievement scores on state and national tests, and well-maintained facilities. They try to survive within a system, not necessarily challenging the status quo.

Currently, in our polarized society educators talk about survival as the goal. Politics have upended curriculum, COVID has upended classrooms and teaching, technology has upended traditional pedagogical practices. Administrators work to navigate the ever-changing landscapes. Such overwhelming uncertainty tends to disincentivize risk-taking behavior. In accordance with the fact that risk-taking is not an attribute districts seek, those who want to create something new, something visionary, are discouraged. People hardly know what the status quo is, let alone how to change it into something else.

Yet in Brunner's work, risk taking was a large part of the professional practice of the women because their working as an administrator in a predominantly male system is inherently risk taking. (Brunner p. 86) Stacey Abrams would say that "We [those she calls outsiders—women and people of color]--aren't going to win playing by the written rules. "The myth of self-made success, or of bold action rewarded for its merits, work in certain circles, but we're not often included in its penumbra." (Abrams, p. 55)

Corollaries of risk-taking are creativity and innovation which are both necessary to create change efforts. To be successful women administrators must balance choosing the right battle with how much risk can they take. For Black women this is especially true. "So, we have to discover the hidden pathways ...to figure out how to circumvent the traditional systems and own opportunity." (Abrams, p. 55)

Brunner found that women administrators who had fathers who treated their female children the way they might treat a boy helped expand the fearlessness it takes to be a risk taker. (Brunner, p. 88)

Being a superintendent is a political position. If any superintendent goes into that position thinking that they can be autonomous and do their own thing, they're misjudging the situation. Risk taking is not part of what they do because the School Board makes just about all the decisions.

For Mary risk taking was **making the best decision at the time with the information you have. And just move on. No second guessing. At least make a decision. I've worked with people who just can't make a decision and that's the worst kind. In a school setting some of those decisions have to be immediate; you don't have time to dwell for weeks or so.**

To avoid taking risks and making risky decisions, some people may use that previously mentioned tactic of appointing a task force or a committee. It is hard for a group to decide. Just talk to trial lawyers about juries!

We had these leadership teams which I'm not sure if they did any good. It was departmental reps and administrators. I actually let my AP run it in our building to give someone else a chance to show some leadership. The purpose of that team was to discuss policies and

practices. They did not make decisions, only recommendations. The [teachers'] Union had a lot of power in terms of some policies and stuff. So power was distributed. (3rd interview, February 16, 2023)

Life Circumstances of Community

Women administrators talk of the need for a supportive community. Early on this is family, bosses, mentors. It may then include women in like positions to share. **In my youth I received a lot of positive affirmation from many, mostly by my teachers. I was supported by my parents too by benign neglect, but my teachers were more actively pushing.**

Mary was raised in a strong family community and neighborhood community. Being segregated demanded that people look out for one another and support each other when possible. Poverty also demanded that people shared what they could. **My family supported me by not denying me anything. Because my mom was there all the time, and my dad was there when he could be. All very supportive. My mom, her support was if you need to do it, just do it.**

They gave me bus money because we didn't have busing. The only time there was busing for Black kids was when my boyfriend lived in a Black housing development without a high school for Black kids. So, the kids were bused into the city to Black schools. They never tried to do busing to get Black kids into white schools and, with

desegregation, everyone knew that white kids were not going to be bused to Black schools.

After laws were passed to force desegregation, the state legislature passed a voucher law to help white families send their kids to private schools. During desegregation a lot of white private schools sprung up. One of my neighbors who was Black, and an attorney, sued and won because his daughter was in a private school, and he wanted to be able to use a voucher. That's when they did away with vouchers because now everyone could get a voucher. They did not want Black families using them.

As far being mentored I learned from working with great principals. I learned by watching some who were not too effective, one, in particular, was a real delegator, meaning he did not do much. He had the cleanest desk I've ever seen of a principal. So I wanted to be a principal because I said to myself, I'm doing all these things [as an AP]; I might as well be a principal because I wrote our equity program and stuff like that. However, another principal was very encouraging and more open-minded.

There was another time I learned from another bad principal. I remember an incident where we were having a Christmas party and I might have been on the social committee. We put invitations in everybody's box, including those of the paras [paraprofessionals]. He was livid. He said, 'No, we don't invite them.' I said, 'What do you mean we don't invite them? They're part of the staff.' 'No, just teachers.' You know, I thought, well, we put invitations in their boxes anyway. I don't believe his way was the way to treat people; they're either a part of the staff or they're not, but you don't distinguish between who can socialize with whom.

Mary also formed relationships with professional colleagues and peers. Plus, her goal, which she accomplished was to establish Central High School itself as a community which was apparent when she opened her back-to-school speech with "We are all in this together."

Life Circumstance of Challenge and Personal Characteristics of courage

Women in Brunner's study said they sought challenges. (Brunner, p. 90) They tested themselves in various situations to see what they could learn from their mistakes and successes.

There were few Black women in this study, perhaps only one. To say that a school administrator had life challenges and courage is redundant when talking about the careers of Black women in white school societies and school systems.

The previous chapters described what it was like for a girl to grow up in a large family in segregated New Orleans, to attend segregated schools and churches. Mary was not wealthy by any means but always had a supportive family. She dealt with getting a college education when there was little money at home to send her, until she got money from her brother and earned scholarships, plus took on low-paid jobs to earn money.

Mary faced racism by her political activism at the height of the Civil Rights Movement. It took a lot of courage to write to and attempt to see the bishop to protest his handling of a white priest in Selma. It took courage for a lone Black girl to work in a Girl Scout camp upstate New York for a summer when she had never attended a camp, let along been in a Jewish camp in upstate New York. It took courage for her to travel by herself to conferences in Washington D.C. and Madison, Wisconsin.

What was a challenge and took a lot of courage was to take a job in Saint Paul Public Schools in the white north and to raise her family here besides. It took courage to face the racism and sexism of being the first Black principal in a major Saint Paul high school when some teachers said they were going to wait to see if she could handle it.

It took courage to challenge policies about sick leave being used for childcare and demanding equal pay to that of a man for the same position.

It was a challenge to become head principal of Central High School with its diverse population and needs and lead that school for 25 years.

Curiosity and Creativity

Brunner describes curiosity embedded with creativity as "the desire to learn more." (Brunner, p. 95) She talks about how creativity is necessary for survival and sometimes squelched by having the uncertainty of risk-taking and not being able to predict the outcome.

When asked about the most creative thing she's ever done, Mary replied, "I remember in sixth grade in middle school I created a whole play. I think it was based on the Biblical story of Job but I had the whole play with characters and dialogue and costumes. I remember that. I was more of a written, creative person. I was in my college play, "You can't Take it With You.—I was the crazy aunt. I was in this Honors Philosophy Class, and we did a play all in white sheets. I once danced in an operetta which is how I got my continuing scholarship to Xavier because they thought I was creative. In middle school I had read a poem standing in front of the whole middle school plus I sang "He's got the Whole World in his Hands."

I've always been curious and as a professional. I always went to workshops, and conventions, to try to learn new things. I didn't come back after every convention and to try to implement something new like some people do, because that turns people off. But we would try certain things that fit our school, our culture, not because it was trendy but because it might help us.

I read a lot—maybe now it's a lot of 'trash' or what's called 'summer reading' but I learn things. I even learned that taking magnesium helps heal leg cramps from a romance novel. [Laughter]

Principle Five: Seeking Retreat

In Brunner's study she probed the way that women used retreat to recharge. She discovered three reasons that happened: 1) to relieve stress and remain physically healthy, 2) to be prepared for all types of situations, 3) to take a break from gender-based difficulties that do not exist for men. (Brunner, p. 101)

Many people use quiet time, exercise, watching movies to take a breather from work. Retreat provides a longer vacation from phone calls and emails and drop-in visits, if people are serious enough to turn off their technology. They can take time to rethink a difficult topic, or refocus priorities or put things in perspective, in general.

Retreating with colleagues can be beneficial in that it allows for professional brainstorming, problem-solving, and support. Yet retreating with friends apart from work colleagues can be beneficial to really put the office on the 'back burner' for a time. Each has a benefit.

Re-entering the workplace after effective time away allows one to regain the strength to meet the daily demands and keep things in perspective.

Mary had her group of women colleagues at St. Paul who would go on retreats to a friend's cabin. **We would listen to each other's stories. Some people would walk. Some would go out in the boat in the** summertime, a little paddle boat. It was getting away from families and the city. We all needed that.

Because we built up this relationship, during the year we'd call each other when we needed to. We are still friends.

Some people take vacations to recharge. **I did not take vacations. I couldn't afford it. The only time I traveled was for business, or for conferences like IB conferences, or principals' conferences. I went down to Costa Rica but that was for IB. Marcee** [daughter] **had just graduated from the University of St. Thomas so she came as her graduation vacation. We never took vacations. My parents never could either. Really with seven kids? No. My dad did not even like driving. Once he was driving and almost drove over a bridge. He never drove again.**

When asked how she stayed healthy, Mary replied, **"I certainly didn't work out. I walked. I walked constantly during the day. At Central I would walk that building many times and mostly just to get the pulse of the climate, figure out what kids were up to and then pass by classrooms to make sure people were engaging kids and not just sitting at their desk. I went to a lot of events, such as basketball and football. I used to lift weights some when Mylo was alive, but mostly my friend and I would go to a club and then lift weights and go have lunch.**

As a retiree I joined the Y and work out on a treadmill and the bike a couple days a week. I stopped during COVID and must start up again. I walk in this house constantly and try to get out to shop, particularly at the thrift stores or grocery store. I'm constantly moving, up and down stairs. Plus, I shovel... [When living in Minnesota, this is a life skill.]

Brunner talked about retreat to stay prepared. Mary did this. **I've always been really good at problem-solving. I don't know why. Even little things around this house will go wrong. I'll say, 'Well, I think I can do this or do that.'** But I remember one of my favorite classes in college was Logic. I always use logic in solving problems or looking at situations. Sometimes I get excited. For example, once there was a little African girl who went crazy in the AP's office; I went crazy right along with her. She was screaming and yelling, and I was screaming and yelling and pounding on the table trying to calm her down. I think I was trying to just tell her I could be as loud and as obnoxious as she was. I was doing it on purpose. It didn't make her stop. She was crazy. When she left Central, she wrote these awful letters saying two of the best English teachers were harassing her. She slandered people which she put all that on Facebook. It was very hurtful.

Principle Six: Compressing Time

Brunner's women realized that every minute counts. Administrative jobs consume many hours a week—twelve to sixteen hours a day. Night meetings. Week-end commitments. It is incumbent to make effective use of time, of every minute, to compress time by making every bit count, which means not wasting time, multi-tasking, delegating, using technology effectively. Sometimes it is difficult to let go and relax because work is the focus of one's thoughts and actions. Sometimes it's hard not to "do", to just be, which is why retreats, exercise, and such practices as meditation are crucial.

Mary, like most administrators who stay healthy in the job, learned ways to take care of herself on the job when the hours were long. **Sometimes I shut the door and put my head down, especially if had a late, late night. Sometimes after school, maybe not during school, I closed my door and told the secretary to give me ten minutes, maybe I'd eat something—potato chips, drink a coke or something. Maybe I'd read a portion of a book I brought with me but not very much. Or I would go to the athletic director's office and chit chat. Or go sit and have coffee with the custodians or go to the kitchen and chit chat with the head nutrition lady. That would recharge me.** (4th interview, March 7, 2023)

Administrative jobs are intense. Plus, many women, like Mary Mackbee, like their jobs. They like being with people, making a difference, helping, learning, feeling like one's life has a purpose. Being an educator is such an honorable profession which is said beautifully in a quote from Parker Palmer, author of <u>Courage to Teach,</u> "I am a teacher at heart, and there are moments in the classroom when I can hardly hold the joy. When my students and I discover uncharted territory to explore, when the pathway out of a thicket opens before us, when our experience is illumined by the lightning-life of the mind—then teaching is the finest work I know." (Palmer, p. 9) Being an administrator is being a teacher and it is one of the finest professions possible.

When asked before she retired what Mary would do, **I am not sure. My work is my life. That's what I have done for so long. Being a principal was the best job. It's why I worked so long. I was afraid to retire, thinking, what am I going to do with myself. My work was my life after my kids.**

As a retiree one gets to set one's own time schedule, which Mary seems to have done handily. **It's been fine. My life is still my kids. I still wash my clothes, engage with my kids but I have more free time. I have bags of books I've read in the last months. I enjoy myself. I do what I want to do. I have breakfast. I had breakfast with a group of teachers last week. I'm going out to dinner with a friend. I still connect because**

I get to hear the latest gossip. (4th interview, March 7, 2023). There are always good books to read especially when one goes to Goodwill and stocks up. There are family commitments, driving to Mateo's restaurant to bring supplies; visiting sick friends; cooking for family. Shoveling.

Doing more than one thing at a time.

Not only do women administrators do and think about more than one thing at a time, but they are also able to deal with a certain amount of "creative disorder" or ambiguity which is a necessary skill when dealing with human beings. Not everything has a definite answer or clear cut.

Earlier it was discussed how Mary organized her time and modeled for her staff that she was organized and got a lot accomplished. She also modeled prioritizing important issues, and downplaying those that were not important. For example, she showed teachers that she valued their time by calling off staff meetings, if there was no need. We all know that a meeting to have a meeting because it's on the calendar eats up a lot of valuable time in anyone's workday.

She also modeled use of time by protecting her private time, particularly on weekends. She attended weekend events and would answer necessary emergencies on weekends, but she was not on email or the telephone over the weekends. Granted, Mary was not a "computer administrator", meaning she did not administer from a computer screen, she believed that people should have family time.

Principle Seven: Exercising Power

It is difficult to define power. Is it power over? Power with? Innate? That all depends on who is having the discussion. Men are more likely to define it as power over; women are more likely to see power as collaborative, power with, which coincides with expected gender roles.

In the 20th century a female theorist, Hannah Arendt, tried to change this stereotypical dynamic by defining power as that "which corresponds to the human ability not just to act but to act in concert. Power is never the property of an individual; it belongs to a group and remains in existence only so long as the group keeps together." (Arendt in Brunner, p. 136) She argued that politics had degenerated into a show of force and violence when in fact it should be a process for "free and equal agents [to] create collective power to create and achieve goals individuals cannot do for themselves." Power then is a "capacity of community of people when they attain their acts of communication, cooperation, and collaboration have been successful." (Arendt in Brunner, p. 136)

Another theorist, Catherine Marshall, stated that "men have been equated with power, while the power women were perceived to have been largely a reflection of the power of the man with or for whom they worked. Women did [do] not have power on their own." (C. Marshall in Brunner, p. 137) Therefore, women leaders in education have struggled with changing the concept of leadership as power over, to power with, which is more in their leadership style and focus. In our increasingly diverse and pluralistic society it is inherent for rigid paradigms to be reworked to meet the needs of a society that is increasingly non-white, multilingual, multicultural, polarized, and technological. The post-#MeToo generation has become increasingly aware of inherent sexual biases and practices and has been less hesitant about reworking some social mores. The heightened awareness of racial bias because of such tragedies as Breonna Taylor and George Floyd make us more alert to racist practices. Yet the studies are still scarce listening to the voices of women and people of color.

Mary Mackbee has managed her way through racism and sexism. **I think power is underrated. Power is what's given. If a staff, for example, does not believe in your abilities and your decisions, then there is no power. Power is relational. It's how you work with your staff, how you involve them. Whether or not you believe that, they have important things to contribute. It's not a dictatorial type of situation, although there are times when, as a leader of a building, you have to make a decision that may not make people happy but usually, if you know your staff and know their values, you can work with them to achieve overall goals. I guess power is working with people, collaboration.**

Sometimes women are not seen as strong as men leaders because they are not as aggressive or assertive. **I can be pretty passive** aggressive when I want, especially with the district, not so much with my staff. With my background, having been at the district for seven years and knowing the politics, I probably was a little more aggressive in terms of dealing with them than the average principal who didn't have that experience because I knew some of the inner workings.

When asked where her power came from, she replied, **I think my power came from my confidence that I could lead the school."** Remember, I came under a cloud. I had been demoted from the district office; I guess I had something to prove that I could still be a good leader. That first year was traumatic because of the riot and rumor of an armed intruder. Central was not an easy place.

My role models showed me that it is important to be fair, honest, and trust your staff. Leah McKenna taught me that. And Dr. Mack J. Spears was fair and very dedicated. He was at that school forever and as a Harvard graduate could have gone anywhere.

When asked about some of the most difficult struggles she had, where she had to demonstrate her power, she replied, **it was when they [the District] made decisions for schools, particularly without our input, like over changing to the seven-period day. They also tried to get rid of our gifted programs, particularly Quest. The fact that they would come in and try to make some decisions to revamp all of our curriculum was not right.**

During this time, I think it was one of the assistant superintendents who said Central had too much. Too much what? Too much of everything.

What we had was a program for everybody. We had the academics; we had the work programs; we had the arts, great band, choir, dance; we had automotive. We had home ec. We kept all of the basics so kids had choices. Other schools were eliminating home ec, and woodshop. They were eliminating the hands-on options. We kept ours because we knew the program well. Our kids had all these varied interests. They weren't just gifted or just IB or Quest or AVID or AP; kids needed life skills too.

We tried to meet the needs of all the students, not just those with high ability.
We wanted to meet the needs of kids with multiple types of abilities. Even the staff said we should be spending money on all the programs, not just IB and AP. We also had the daycare program for a while.

Central had the first in-house daycare program in the state and it was run by the District. Other schools had daycare programs run by organizations like Children's Home Society which is one of the reasons ours closed because it was too expensive because the District actually paid the going wage. But it was open for over 30 years. There was some good news when it closed because the girls were not getting pregnant. There are still programs for pregnant teens, however.

The whole idea of power is interesting. You can't run a school by yourself. You've got to trust the people. As an administrator you hire people with skills you lack so that you can depend on them to help you. You don't have to know everything or do everything. If someone is good with technology, use their skills. You don't have to learn everything yourself. Some people are good at organizing—let them build the schedule; some are good with technology, let them deal with cameras.

The female principals I know were strong, strong leaders but they weren't like a Tsarina. Although one kid, I do have this picture, thought I was dictatorial because we would impose rules. He posted pictures around the school with my face in a Russian tsar's body and they called me "Tsarina."

I suppose they thought I was a dictator, but I have an example when I wasn't, one of many, when kids actually helped make the decisions. I did have run-ins with kids about issues, but this was an example of how we solved it together. We had a Homecoming Court which was always presented at an assembly in the gym. Before the event we would go over appropriate dress and stuff like that. The day of the Court this young boy came dressed as a girl. I said he had had been at the meeting when they had gone over appropriate dress. He said he had but he wanted to wear the dress. I looked at the rest of the

Court and said, 'It's your decision. You can decide whether or not if he can go like that. I just left. They decided he could go. I thought he was making a mockery of the proceedings. It wasn't about him being gay or trans, but it seemed he was just mocking the event. The kids said to let him go and I said, 'Fine.' Choose your battles.

Today this discussion would be a moot point with the LGTBQ+ awareness. But it proves that the true use of power is to recognize that a current practice or rule may need to change, modified, or abandoned. Enforcing a rule just because it's always been done flies in the face of our changing society. Sometimes there is good reason to enforce a standard; sometimes it is very reasonable to change.

Mary also demonstrated the collaborative nature of power—she distributed the authority to those directly involved in the process, demonstrating her leadership style.

One value that was a guiding principle for Mary was in making certain people showed respect for Central High School, recognizing that wherever they went under the name of Central, they were presenting an image to the public of what the high school stood for. **I told them wherever you are it is an extension of the school. You are representing the school. You need to act and be appropriate.** That rule did not change.

In Brunner's study some women said that their use of power was sometimes tempered by their fear of criticism of being too strong or too like a man. Was that true for Mary? **I think I was strong, which was probably my background. I was raised in a family of five boys which helped; I went to all Black schools where the principals were hands-on and not afraid to get physical with kids. I was competitive whether playing poker or softball in the field and in school. I don't look at power as power; I look at power as leadership. I don't think they are mutually exclusive, but one seems more negative than the other.**

Practical Leadership in Action

This is the important part. How does one put it all together to use theories of leadership combined with a person's skills and experiences to be an effective leader, especially now when so much has changed drastically with our current political climate and post-COVID? How does one become a leader for the future?

Few books discuss the ins and outs of day-to-day leadership to give practical advice and share effective practices, especially for those future leaders who are not white men. Stacey Abrams in <u>Lead from the Outside: How to Build your Future and Make Real Change</u> is an exception. Her book speaks especially to those she called "outsiders" for whom "race, gender, class have been constant markers of access, beginning with the Constitution. She wanted to "deconstruct the successes and failures I had and distill them into potential guidelines for others." (Abrams, p. ix) Plus, as minorities move closer to parity, we have to be ready to lead beyond what we might imagine." (Abrams, p. xxiii) However, her advice is practical for all modern leaders in this time of change. It would be a great book to use in university courses on leadership by providing practical examples and opportunities for case studies and role plays.

With each chapter Abrams explores a topic, such as "Dare to want More", or "Fear and Otherness", which give personal examples of how she and others have dealt with the topic, plus she provides tools for a reader to examine their own practices and set goals to do something different. This is not a pitch to sell her book; it is, however, a recognition that this book provides wisdom unseen and unheard of in other books.

There are examples throughout the book that could be cited here, but there are two that are particularly noteworthy. One, she redefines the idea of mentors and, two, she describes Work-Life Jenga.

Courses in universities and books on leadership discuss the need for and values of having a mentor. However, in those discussions the actual role of the mentor and the concurrent role of the person being mentored is rarely discussed. Yet in Sigford's study of high school principals, they all said they had mentors. But their idea of a mentor was that person who said perhaps only once said that "????? [insert name here] you should go into administration." What women administrators found was that the most support came from finding and using a group of job-alikes which was difficult in rural areas. Plus, finding a cadre of women can even more difficult, particularly if looking for a cadre of women of color in job-alike situations.

In her chapter The Myth of Mentors, Abrams said,

> "I don't have traditional mentors, Instead I have curated support, training, and advise e from an array of alliances, advisers, and friends: an a la care approach designed for maximum input and flexibility, for a range of circumstances that can defy the conventional wisdom of success. Minority leaders—like everyone in charge—need help and lots of it, from my experience. We need guidance, redirection, a sounding board, and correction. But we also have to learn to excavate our whole experience to find the right people to help us along. First, we have to understand what we're looking for—a counselor or a gatekeeper who sneaks us inside or a phone-a-friend who knows the right answers. Eventually, most of us will need all of the above. The trick is knowing what you need and making the right asks. (Abrams, p. 2)

Abrams emphasized that the myth of a single mentor is not productive. One needs different things at different times. "Business books and magazine articles extol the virtue of mentors without really explaining that the responsibility for the relationship is on the mentee. For people of color, women, and those just starting out, in particular, there's a strong benefit to having a mentor to help navigate uncharted area. If a mentor is what you want, then you must be clear about what you need." (p. 83)

She even provides a list of the types of mentors one needs, which she renames as a "board of advisers." First, there is a sponsor who can open doors and speak for you. Next there is an adviser who offers more consistent advice over a longer period of time. Third, situational advisors are most likely around subject-matter expertise. Fourth, are peer advisors who are similar in age or positions. (Abrams, p. 101)

Without knowing it, Mary has used different advisers. As a young woman she had mentors who stimulated her to become an educator, even suggesting becoming a social studies teacher; some helped her get scholarships and facilitated admission into college. She had situational advisors with people like Dr. Neal Nickerson who helped her grow with her knowledge of educational administration. Plus, she developed a cadre of women administrators, not necessarily principals, whom she used for emotional support, opportunities for relaxation, and for problem-solving. There were many along the way, but she, like many, never had one person who was there for a long time for all purposes. Business literature needs to change its ideas of mentoring.

The other poignant take-away from Abrams was her chapter on Work-Life Jenga as she discredits the ideas that there is such a thing as work-life balance. "I reject the idea of work-life balance." Abrams suggests that there are no tips or tricks that "create a lifestyle equilibrium." (p. 175). She believes in Work-Life Jenga like the game of Jenga where one tries to stack same-size pieces into a stack and then tries to make moves without destroying the tower. However, "In Work-Life Jenga, the expectation is not one of balance; it's one of strategy and making the best of each move, one block at a time." (Abrams, p. 175) To do this, she operates under five rules: one, life comes first; two, don't deal with jerks; three, only take projects that engage the head and the heart; four, if it can't change the world, don't do it; and five, sleep is optional.   (Abrams, p. 185)

Mary did not read Abrams' book but her style could be considered Jenga-like. She kept trying to "build the tower" and if it started to collapse, she rebuilt it and started over. For Mary life comes first in her belief that she makes decisions based on what is good for her family, for the students, teachers, and school community. She did not spend time on "jerks". If a teacher was not doing their job, she provided coaching. If that didn't work, she helped them move on, either to retirement or a different career. She also does not waste time on people or things that are "cup half empty" people. It is impossible to ever fill that cup. The projects Mary worked on her entire life were her family, her school family, her community both growing up and as an adult. Projects that involve the head and the heart are those that enhance the opportunities and lives of those she knows. As for sleep, sometimes that's difficult.

Conclusion: It's about the Person

What is important to remember is what counts is the person in the leadership role. Theories are just that—theories--but the person who puts the action into them as a product of their life experiences, challenges and hurdles is demonstrating leadership. We lead who we are.

This chapter explored the concept of leadership from the perspective of societal sexism and racism, from abstract sometimes scholarly research on the concept of leadership, from practical applications for real life practitioners. We heard Mary's definition of leadership and explored two practical applications from Stacy Abrams' practical advice for those "outside" the penumbra of privilege.

What if the studies of leadership focused more on the person, the WHO and then the WHERE. Not every person can be successful in every situation. The person is strategic but so is the context of their work. It is the synergy of WHO and WHERE that makes leadership.

Particularly, as we move forward into a rapidly changing society and changing expectations of education, it is important to recognize that leadership is a personal skill, the ability to stack the "Jenga" and rebuild it when it does not stand up. Thanks, Ms. Abrams.

CHAPTER EIGHT

What made Mary Mackbee such a good Leader

What makes Mary M. Mackbee a person who led in the past but is a role model for leaders of the future?

For her legacy she said that **the only thing I would want people to say is that I cared about people, students, staff, and parents. That I tried to do the best job I could. One thing is that in the view of all those people who helped me, who mentored me, and whom I try to emulate, they believe I've done a good job trying to follow in their footsteps. I'm talking about my own administrators in my growing up years—my own teachers. They were the ones who inspired me. Those at Valena C. Jones, Rivers Fredrick, McDonough 35, and Xavier University.** (W-H. 124)

That statement is a recognition that one's life experiences can be an important predictor of the future person. It's testament to the power of teachers and administrators, to the need for strong role models, to the power of having men and women of color in management positions, to the legacy of learning from strong teachers to the truth in Mary's belief that education is freedom. Strong teachers and administrators cannot be replaced by a computer or ipad. People and relationships are key.

Mary also changed over time by taking the good from the past and tweaking it as things change. Some ideas have longevity, such as the admonition to Central students that when they are in public, they are representing the school and must behave accordingly. Others, such as restrictions about what clothing is appropriate for boys and girls must change. Therefore, leadership takes skills and knowledge to be wrapped in personal strengths and attributes.

Mary is a role model as a leader of the future because she demonstrated that the use of power is also the use of flexibility. It may be too simplistic, but it would be illuminating if one would take a checklist of Mary's attributes and gave it to hiring committees when they are looking for future educational leaders so that the personal attributes are given as much credibility as management factoids.

Here is a fun attempt to create a list of the many characteristics of Mary's leadership although they are not in any particular order. Imagine having this in your hand during an interview when hiring future administrators.

- ☐ Intelligent
- ☐ Ethical
- ☐ Decisive decision-maker
- ☐ Willing and skilled listener
- ☐ Relationship-builder
- ☐ Commitment to people
- ☐ Hard-working
- ☐ Risk-taker

- ☐ Non-judgmental
- ☐ Non-sexist
- ☐ Non-racist
- ☐ Non-homophobe
- ☐ Has sense of humor
- ☐ Has common sense
- ☐ Does the right thing for the right reason (What's good for people.)
- ☐ Reads
- ☐ Constantly learns
- ☐ Understands need for healthy management practices
- ☐ Understands and maintains budgets and financial processes
- ☐ Delegator
- ☐ Good Cook
- ☐ Family-oriented
- ☐ Community builder
- ☐ Educated
- ☐ Team builder
- ☐ Effective time manager
- ☐ Believes education is freedom
- ☐ Fighter, when necessary
- ☐ Organized
- ☐ Logical
- ☐ Multi-tasker
- ☐ Tolerant of creative chaos
- ☐ Can unravel ambiguity
- ☐ Doesn't smoke
- ☐ Generous with time, money, and herself
- ☐ Loyal
- ☐ Fair—believes in justice
- ☐ Humble
- ☐ Intentionally mentors others
- ☐ Courageous
- ☐ Inspirational
- ☐ Capacity Builder

☐ Even-tempered

There are probably things that have been omitted. But this is a starting point.

Yes, I can be replaced. It may not be me, and it may not be the same, but there is somebody who is just as dedicated, just as compassionate, and who can do the job. There are people who are just like me. They may do things differently; I would never think that I was so special that I couldn't be replaced—I don't People say, 'You can't leave' I say, 'You know, everybody is replaceable. I don't think I'm irreplaceable.' If I die tomorrow, somebody will be in this office the next day taking over. They may not do it like me, but that doesn't mean that they're going to do any less. They'll do it in their own way. (W-H, p. 123)

Mary's story is an important one.

CHAPTER NINE
Currently

Mary retired in 2019 after 25 years at Central and 52 years in the Saint Paul Public Schools.

She is still in her house in Bloomington. She is still the matriarch of her family with various family members staying with her at times. Some people have asked her about that and she says it's probably a cultural things, multi-age groups living together from time to time and during times when people needed a place to be. As she says, **Even now, if I have extra money it goes to my kids for whatever—extra diapers, extra formula for the new baby or winter coats for my four other grandchildren. I'll help my kids.** (Wilcox-Harris, p. 90)

This author has a personal addition to that story. I was lucky enough to be an assistant principal to Mary for four years. When I started in St. Paul, contract negotiations were taking place. I was placed on the salary schedule at a lower rate from where I had left. I too was a single mother. After settlement when the back pay checks came out, I had seven dollars less. I didn't understand why, but I was in tears. Mary knew I was upset; she took me out for coffee. She said that she understood and that she even had a "cash flow problem." Knowing what I did about how Mary helped kids at

Central when they needed it, her own kids, and friends, I replied to her, "You don't have a cash flow problem; you have a cash stoppage problem." We laughed. The point being is that Mary is generous and feels committed to her family, recognizing that we all need a little help now and then.

Not only does she host family members to stay with her, but she often hosts family pets, one or two dogs or cats. They all like coming to "Grandma's" house.

What does she do in retirement? Read a lot for one thing. She often has bags of books to return to Goodwill and she will fill those bags back up to bring home a new selection.

Luckily, she was not working full-time during the height of COVID. Plus, St. Paul calls her to be an administrative sub when an administrator gets COVID, has a death in the family, and so on. She has seen a difference in the kids since COVID. They have little respect for school or school personnel. When Mary tries to get middle school kids into class and out of the halls, they tell her there is nothing she can do to them; they really don't have to go to school until high school when it counts. Parents have not been helpful to support the fact that their children need to participate in learning. She has definitely seen the discipline issues and mental health changes that one reads about in the newspaper.

When asked what she sees as remedies, she is as bewildered and confused as current practitioners because it's a very different environment and it feels like there are fewer options.

However, Mary's story and accomplishments demonstrate a person who learned about leadership in many ways. Her longevity and success suggest that she was able to maintain relationships and educational integrity. Her personal skills have helped, along with the supportive staff and community, a school that has maintained its academic reputation and continues its programming that looks forward to a more complicated future, one rife with rapid change.

She is truly a model to emulate for educational leaders of the future.

Mary's "Bobblehead" she received as a gift

Mary and Snoopy: Charles Schulz was Central Graduate

ABOUT THE AUTHOR

Jane L. Sigford has spent her career as a lifelong educator, starting as an Englis teacher and later becoming a teacher of learning disabled and behavioral/emotionally disturbed students. Her administrative career began as a dean of students, then an Assistant Principal of Central High School where I met Mary Mackbee, then as a high school principal, and retiring from the exciting position as Executive Director of Curriculum and Instruction for the Wayzata Public Schools.

In addition, she has been an adjunct professor at two universities in the Mpls/St. Paul communities. Her work as a professional developer has given her the opportunity to work with educators across the region and around the United States.

She has published *Who Said School Administration would be Fun* which had two editions, and *The School Leader's Guide to Management* published by Corwin Press.

She was fortunate to work with MASA, Minnesota Association of School Administrators as a Thought Leader for the Aspiring Superintendents Academy, as a podcaster, and as a book reviewer.

She has a B.A. in English Education, a Master of Arts in English with a focus on Black literature, and an Ed.D. in Educational Leadership from the University of Minnesota.

She, like many, has been fortunate to be mentored by some wonderful educators. As an acknowledgement of their work, she has chosen to write two books about two of the most powerful in her career. Her first memoir was *Id' Do it All Over Again"* about Dr. Neal Nickerson Jr., professor from the University of Minnesota who held the recognition of helping the successful completion of more doctorate degrees than any professor in the United States, at one time.

However, this latest memoir of Mary M. Mackbee has been a joy to write about the most ethical administrator I have ever had the pleasure of working with. She is more than a mentor to me—she has become a dear friend

BIBLIOGRAPHY

Abrams, Stacey. (2019). Lead from the Outside: How to Build your Future and Make Real Change. New York: Picador.

Brunner, C.Cryss. (2000). Principles of Power: Women Superintendents and the Riddle of the Heart. Albany: State University of New York Press.

"Efforts to ban Critical Race Theory" (Retrieved April 16, 2023). Education Week. https://www.edweek.org/leadership/efforts-to-ban-critical-race-theory-now-restrict-teaching-for-a-third-of-americas-kids/2022/

"Famous quotes of Shirley Chisholm". (Retrieved April 14, 2023). Quote Fancy. https://linksinc.org/the-links-incorporated/#:~:text=the%20United%20Kingdom.

"Five common leadership styles, and how to find your own." (Retrieved April 20, 2023), WeWork. https://www.google.com/search?q=five+types+of+leadership&oq=five+types+of+leadership&aqs=chrome..69i57j0i512j0i22i30l8.8284j0j7&sourceid=chrome&ie=UTF-8

Fields, Gary. (2023, April 16, 2023) "Democracy for U.S. Blacks is being threatened, report says." *Minneapolis Star and Tribune*. A8.

"Florida Ban on AP African American Studies". (Retrieved April 16, 2023). Education Week. https://www.edweek.org/teaching-learning/floridas-ban-on-ap-african-american-studies-explained/2023

"Hate Crime Statistics 2021". (Retrieved April 16, 2023). Department of Justice. https://linksinc.org/the-links-incorporated/#:~:text=the%20United%20Kingdom.

"Land-grant university" (Retrieved April 8, 2023). Wikipedia. https://en.wikipedia.org/wiki/Land-grant_university.

Lorenz-Meyer, Elizabeth and N. Wagner. (2016). Onward Central: the First 150 Years of St. Paul

Central High School . Blue Stem Heritage Group.

Mistretta, Anne Marie and P. Phillips. (1987). Profile of a Principal—Blending Multiple Roles for Success. NASSP Bulletin, 117-121.

"Poems by Paul Laurence Dunbar", (Retrieved April 19, 2023) GetLit, https://getlitanthology.org/poemdetail/373/

"New Roads, Louisiana".(Retrieved April 5, 2023). Louisiana, https://ww"w.louisianatravel.com/cities/new- roads.

"Race and Segregation in St. Paul Public Schools" (Retrieved April 12, 2023). Minnesota State Historical Society. https://www.mnhs.org/education/resources/race-and-segregation-st-pauls-public-schools#:~:text=Paul%20schools%20side%2Dby%2Dside,remained%20in%20force%20until%201869.,

"Saint Paul Central High School", (Retrieved April 19, 2023). Wikipedia. https://en.wikipedia.org/wiki/Saint_Paul_Central_High_School#History.

Schweiger, Sylvia, et. al. (2020) Barriers to Leadership development: Why is it so difficult to Abandon the hero. Leadership, 16(4), 411-433.

Sigford, Jane L. (1995). Self-Determinants of Success to the Women who are Head Principals of High Schools. Unpublished doctoral dissertation, University of Minnesota, Minneapolis.

Sigford, Jane L. (1998) "Message Bearer" Unpublished Paper.

"The Links, Incorporated" (Retrieved April 13, 2023). Links Incorporated. https://linksinc.org/the-links-incorporated/#:~:text=the%20United%20Kingdom.

Tatum, Beverly. (2017). *Why Are the Black Kids Sitting Together in the Cafeteria.* New York: Basic Books.

Wilcox-Harris, Kathleen Marie. (2009). A Great Capacity to Love: A Life of Mary Morrell Mackbee. Unpublished doctoral dissertation, University of St. Thomas.

Young, Claudia K. (1976). Women in School Administration and Supervision: A New Leadership Dimension. <u>NASSP Bulletin,</u> 60 (400), 83-87.

Made in the USA
Monee, IL
27 December 2023